YEMEN

WHAT EVERYONE NEEDS TO KNOW®

YEMEN

WHAT EVERYONE NEEDS TO KNOW®

ASHER ORKABY

OXFORD
UNIVERSITY PRESS

OXFORD
UNIVERSITY PRESS

Oxford University Press is a department of the University of Oxford. It furthers the University's objective of excellence in research, scholarship, and education by publishing worldwide. Oxford is a registered trade mark of Oxford University Press in the UK and certain other countries.

"What Everyone Needs to Know" is a registered trademark of Oxford University Press.

Published in the United States of America by Oxford University Press 198 Madison Avenue, New York, NY 10016, United States of America.

© Oxford University Press 2021

Library of Congress Cataloging-in-Publication Data
Names: Orkaby, Asher, author.
Title: Yemen : what everyone needs to know / Asher Orkaby.
Description: New York, NY : Oxford University Press, [2021] |
Series: What everyone needs to know | Includes index.
Identifiers: LCCN 2020029569 (print) | LCCN 2020029570 (ebook) |
ISBN 9780190932268 (hardback) | ISBN 9780190932275 (paperback) |
ISBN 9780190932299 (epub)
Subjects: LCSH: Yemen (Republic)—History. |
Yemen (Republic)—Politics and government. |
Classification: LCC DS247.Y48 O74 2021 (print) |
LCC DS247.Y48 (ebook) | DDC 953.3—dc23
LC record available at https://lccn.loc.gov/2020029569
LC ebook record available at https://lccn.loc.gov/2020029570

1 3 5 7 9 8 6 4 2

Paperback printed by LSC Communications, United States of America
Hardback printed by Bridgeport National Bindery, Inc., United States of America

To my mother, for teaching me how to tell—and retell—a story.

CONTENTS

LIST OF MAPS

ACKNOWLEDGMENTS

It seems, at times, that Yemen exists in two different realities. The Yemen I grew up with is defined by its long history, linguistic heritage, culinary delights, unique architecture, and industrious and creative population. The Yemen of contemporary media is portrayed as a perpetual war zone, a humanitarian crisis, a sectarian tragedy, and a battlefield for the Saudi-Iranian rivalry. How does one reconcile these two realities in a book that ambitiously proposes to share *what everyone needs to know about Yemen*? It starts with first determining who "everyone" is and what questions they have about Yemen. Then one sits down with fellow Yemenis and other experts in the field to answer those questions in a fashion that combines these two seemingly opposing visions of Yemen in a coherent narrative that can serve as a foundation for future informal discussions of what *else* everyone needs to know about Yemen.

This multitude of perspectives was gleaned not only from my own research both in Yemen and in archives around the world, but also from conversations over dinner, non-Yemeni coffee, and social media. While the anonymous voices of hundreds of Yemenis can be found in the pages of this book, I would like to thank a few individuals in particular for reading portions of it and for consulting with me on a number of contentious Yemen topics: Khlood al-Hagar, Afrah Nasser, Safa Karman, Abdo al-Bahesh, Bernard Haykel, Adam Baron, Tawakol Karman, Maysaa Shujaa, Elisabeth Kendall, Ahmed bin Mubarak, James L. Gelvin, Gregory Johnsen, Charles Dunbar, Les Campbell, Leonard Wood, Alsoswa Amat, Thanos Petouris,

Christopher Ward, H. Arnold Sherman, Golzar Sepehri, Farhad Dokhani, and Tarek Abu Hussein.

Obtaining permission to reproduce a few lines of beautiful Yemeni poetry was no easy task. A particular thanks to Daniel Varisco, Samuel Liebhaber, and Salem Baafi. Thank you as well to David McBride, Holly Mitchell, Liz Davey, and the rest of the extended Oxford University Press editorial staff.

Productive writing cannot be done from just anywhere. A special thanks to Princeton University's Transregional Institute, Harvard University's Davis Center, and the Wilson Center for providing a conducive intellectual environment in which I was able to research, write, and edit this manuscript.

Words cannot describe the debt of gratitude that I have for my loving wife Ariela who, even while running a COVID unit in the hospital, managed to help me carve out the hours needed to complete this book, and even found the time to read over every chapter and make sure that I was still using proper English grammar after weeks immersed in Yemeni Arabic sources. And to my delightful children for at least pretending that they were interested in my tales from Yemen and for agreeing to replace bedtime stories with soporific Ancient History narratives.

INTRODUCTION

My country is handed over from one tyrant to the next, a worse
  tyrant;
from one prison to another, from one exile to another.
It is colonized by the observed invader and the hidden one;
handed over by one beast to two, like an emaciated camel.
In the caverns of its death my country neither dies nor recovers.
It digs in the muted graves looking for its pure origins, for its spring-
  time promise that slept behind its eyes for the dream that will
  come, for the phantom that hid.
It moves from one overwhelming night to a darker night.
My country grieves in its own boundaries and in other people's land
and even on its own soil suffers the alienation of exile.
  —Abdullah al-Baradouni (1929–1999), "From Exile to Exile"

On March 21, 1942, a son was born to a poor family in the village of
Beit al-Ahmar near Yemen's capital city of Sana'a. His father, who
had worked as the village blacksmith, died at an early age leaving
the orphaned boy to be raised by his mother. Every dry season, the
family moved from village to village in search of grazing land for
their small flock of sheep. The task of tending these sheep was given
to the young boy. Local educators discovered him to be a precocious
student with a talent for memorizing religious texts and writing. At
the age of 12, he left home to go visit his older brother in the army
barracks south of their village. So enamored was he by the comrade-
ship of the army that he lied about his age and enlisted. Driven by

personal ambition and love for his Yemeni homeland, he dedicated his life to the army and was selected to join the officer's school in 1960, paving the way to military and political leadership. The character in this story of rags to riches, who was able to rise above deep personal tragedy, was none other than the notorious Ali Abdullah Saleh, Yemen's former president and the individual who had the most profound impact on the modern state of Yemen.

Over the course of his 33-year presidency, Saleh crafted the modern Yemeni state, which was built on precarious foundations of tribal agreements, temporary truces, negotiated boundaries, political nepotism and patronage, and widespread corruption. Only Saleh understood the intricacies of his own creation and, as the country discovered, after he stepped down from the presidency in 2012, only Saleh could control all its moving elements. His alliance with the Houthi rebels in 2014 was the ultimate betrayal for the last remnants of Yemeni society that still revered him as a revolutionary leader. As president, he was a mirror of Yemeni society, exuding optimism in the early 1990s and marking the first stages of the country's gradual decline a decade later, a consequence of Saleh's mismanagement and exploitation of Yemeni resources for his own personal gain. The story of modern Yemen is, in part, the biography of its longest serving president, but it is also the story of a historic people with a rich culture, religious tradition, language, and heritage. Even before Saleh's death in December 2017, the Yemeni people and their remaining leadership have struggled to redefine their country whose borders, politics, and tensions were so closely tied to the presidency of one man. This book will trace the country's history, society, economy, and politics, to present a comprehensive picture of what everyone needs to know about Yemen.

Summarizing the centuries

Bab al-Mandeb, the waterway connecting the Red Sea to the Indian Ocean, has been both a blessing and a curse for the southwest corner of South Arabia known as Yemen. Centuries of history have demonstrated that under the right leadership, Yemen could transform into a regional power and an epicenter for global trade as it did during the ancient Sabean Kingdom when the world looked to

Yemen for its supply of frankincense. History has also shown that without central leadership, South Arabia will be overrun by regional powers looking to control this vital waterway and secure an important asset for global trade.

The country, however, is not merely a bystander of global commerce and regional power dynamics. As one of the oldest centers of civilizations in the Near East, Yemen has archeological riches and architecturally distinctive mudbrick buildings that have been labeled World Heritage sites by the United Nations Educational, Scientific, and Cultural Organization (UNESCO). The capital city of Sana'a, in particular, one of the oldest continuously settled cities in the world, features an old city that transports visitors to 14th-century Arabia with authentic spice markets, Arabic dialects whose speakers take pride in their linguistic authenticity, and a rich oral tradition of poetry and song. Two religious sects dominate the social landscape: Zaydi Islam, a small sect of Shi'i Islam found in the northern highlands, and the Sunni Islam sect of Shafi'i Islam on the western coast and southern regions. Other Islamic groups, in addition to small communities of Christians, Jews, and Bahais, can be found across the country, each maintaining their own unique history.

Yemen's topography is as diverse as its history, featuring a flat coastal plain in the west, mountains across the north and center, a vast desert to the east, and an archipelago off the southern coast famous for its biodiversity. In an Arabian Peninsula known for its deserts and oil, Yemen stands out as the regional breadbasket, the birthplace of coffee, and the world's capital of *qat*, a narcotic leaf chewed by most of the population. Agricultural produce was once exported by land over Arabian camel caravans and by sea through the southern port city of Aden, one of the world's largest natural harbors. It was Aden that often repeatedly attracted the attention of modern colonial powers, from the 16th-century Portuguese Empire to multiple Ottoman imperial forays into South Arabia, and finally the 19th-century British seizure of Aden.

Throughout the centuries, dating back to at least the 14th century, Sana'a and the northern highlands were controlled by an *imam*, a central religious authority who oversaw the local dynamics of tribal federations and alliances. The Yemeni imamate lasted until 1962 when a modern republic was founded in North Yemen. The new republic overthrew a centuries-old social hierarchy based on Zaydi religious principles and the *sayyid* families, or those who could trace their genealogy to the prophet Muhammad. Replacing the imam were a succession of presidents, most of whom were military figures, supported by a cadre of Yemenis who were educated abroad and returned to Yemen to lead their country into the modern era. Presidential succession culminated with the rise of Ali Abdullah Saleh in 1979, setting the stage for three decades of power consolidation, corruption, and neglected development.

The southern half of Yemen gained independence from the British Empire in 1967 and formed the first and only Arab communist state. The Soviet Union and China became proprietors of South Yemen's People's Democratic Republic of Yemen, which simultaneously remained an outcast in intra-Arab politics and a haven for international terrorist organizations and revolutionary movements. Political tensions between different southern factions impeded economic development and often caused friction with the Yemen Arab Republic to the north. This socialist haven in Arabia, a beacon of education, gender equality, and communist ideology, was, however, reliant upon external financing and was driven to bankruptcy when the Soviet Union pulled out of the developing world.

Following the end of the Cold War, North and South Yemen unified in 1990, forming the Republic of Yemen, which constitute the contemporary borders and governing institutions of the modern state of Yemen. Tensions between the newly unified countries erupted in a 1994 civil war, a manifestation of southern resentment of northern domination. Southern grievances continue to fester nearly three decades later as the call for South Yemen independence has grown. The foundation of the al-Hirak southern movement in 2007 and the Southern Transitional Council in 2017 have given political form to public protest and calls for independence.

Similar grievances exist between the republican capital of Sana'a and the northern tribes formerly affiliated with the pre-1962 ruling imam and today known by the common name of the Houthi movement. Post-revolutionary Yemen during the 1970s–1990s sought to transform the former imamate into a modern republic by diminishing the role of the country's northern tribes and scaling back the influence of Zaydi ideology in Yemen. These national policies, along with Saudi religious proselytization in northern Yemen, has flamed the anti-Sana'a sentiments. A series of six inconclusive wars between the Yemeni government and the Houthis (2004–2010) culminated in the 2014 Houthi capture of Sana'a and the onset of the current crisis. The arrival of the Arab Spring protests in Yemen in 2011 precipitated the downfall of Ali Abdullah Saleh, who had been Yemen's president for 33 years and whose administration was most responsible for the declining state of Yemen's economy, politics, and social infrastructure. Mansur Hadi replaced Saleh in 2012, overseeing the National Dialogue Conference that convened a cross-section of Yemeni society to craft a new constitution and form a new post-Saleh national government. The optimism of post–Arab Spring Yemen quickly faded as the revolution was hijacked by Sana'a political elites who were blind to continued Houthi military expansion. By the time Sana'a was captured in 2014, it was too late to save the new government, the members of which were forced to flee to Riyadh and seek the assistance of Saudi Arabia in defeating the Houthi rebellion.

True to its historical form, Yemen has since been overrun by regional power rivalries: Iran has emerged as a supporter of the Houthi movement while Saudi Arabia, Yemen's neighbor to the north, has organized an extensive military operation and blockade to defend the country's deposed republican government. The ongoing war has placed Yemen's 28 million residents in the crosshairs of a man-made humanitarian crisis. International peace efforts have been ineffectual, and the country has entered a debilitating stalemate with all sides entrenched in their positions and no single political entity capable of keeping the country together.

Deconstructing generalizations

Yemen is often referred to by the media as a "failed state," with experts citing the absence of a central governing authority and the prevalence of regional competition for power among local tribal figures, complicated by the presence of international groups using the amorphous title of al-Qaeda. There are some countries, like Egypt, that cannot exist without either the state, or an equivalent central national organization that unites disparate groups. Yemen, on the other hand, does not need to exist as a centralized state as nearly every aspect of economic, political, religious, and social life has, and continues to be, dominated by local tribal identities and codes of conduct. For centuries, foreign powers and kingdoms did not occupy or control territory in Yemen but rather arrived at temporary mutually beneficial understandings with local tribal sheikhs, overseen by a weak and decentralized governing structure. Referring to Yemen as a "failed state" is an inherently flawed perception that imposes Western notions of state structure in a region dominated by tribal, territorial, and familial forms of government that predate the emergence of the European modern state.

Western media have similarly dismissed Yemen as another battleground in the Saudi-Iranian rivalry or the doctrinal split between Sunni and Shi'i branches of Islam. There is no long-standing history of sectarian conflict in Yemen, although it is a deeply religious country without strict boundaries between politics, religion, and tribal dynamics. There is, however, a long history of Saudi-Yemeni tension related to border security and three disputed territories. Iran, on the other hand, had little interaction with this southwest corner of the Arabian Peninsula prior to 2015. The current civil war in Yemen is not a conflict between two opposing regional hegemons; rather, it is a culmination of 70 years of political and social tensions and gradual transformations within tribal and social hierarchies.

The majority of political opinion has wrongly depicted the Houthi movement as an Iranian terrorist proxy that has invaded and conquered Yemen. The Houthis constitute an alliance of northern tribes united by adherence to a shared religious identity and disdain for the government in Sana'a. The movement is a struggle for religious freedom, political rights, and social equality by a minority of the population that has been living in the northern highlands for over a thousand years. Rather than a contemporary band of foreign interlopers, the Houthi movement is the culmination of a decades-long struggle between a marginalized population and the Yemeni government. Recent external influence on the Houthi movement does not emanate from Tehran directly, but has been outsourced to Hezbollah in Lebanon where the Houthi media and propaganda strategy are based. Iran's greatest impact on the Houthi movement has been indoctrinating its leadership with extremist religious ideology and training their civil service in guerilla warfare and propaganda, featuring the infamous slogan: "Death to America! Death to Israel! Curse upon the Jews and Victory for Islam!"

The recent discussion of the humanitarian crisis in Yemen, a country that most Westerners can scarcely find on a map, has fostered a misperception that Yemen has always been impoverished, is mostly desert, and is in a remote area inconsequential to world events. In fact, Yemen is one of the oldest settled regions in the world. Its territory abuts the strait of Bab al Mandeb, one of the world's most important waterways, that has placed Yemen at the crossroads of both major historic trade routes and millennia of regional struggle to control the strategic and lucrative territory. Yemen is unique among the countries of the Arabian Peninsula because of its fertile agricultural land and picturesque terraced gardens that once made South Arabia fabulously wealthy. Recent stories of conflict and terrorism have far overshadowed Yemen's vibrant, educated, and active civil society.

The modern Yemeni state was founded in 1962 by a group of foreign-educated Yemenis who returned home to replace the country's thousand-year theocracy with a modern republic. This educated elite constituted the core of Yemen's civil service, public education, and university leadership until the 2000s when nepotism, corruption, and economic recession dissuaded a new generation of expatriates from returning home and taking up the mantle of the post-revolutionary generation. Although Yemeni civil society organizations continue to play an important role in promoting women's rights, child welfare laws, anti-corruption, poverty reduction, and animal rights, areas such as freedom for women concerning clothing, socializing, marriage, and other rights are tightly controlled by a powerful religious elite. Nevertheless, a small number of Yemeni women have risen to prominence despite living in a restrictive and religiously conservative society.

As the Arab Spring protests captivated audiences across the world, many, including Yemen's burgeoning and disaffected youth, assumed that the country was on the path to true democracy. Street protests eventually led to the ousting of President Ali Abdullah Saleh, followed by a great deal of optimism surrounding the transitional government. However, as was the case across most of the Middle East, the Arab Spring brought neither democracy nor freedom. Rather, the fall of a dictator opened the gates to a multitude of militant groups, previously on the radical fringe of mainstream politics, and led to the beginning of Yemen's current civil war.

The war in Yemen is not a struggle between regional powers or religious sects but a domestic conflict between political, social, tribal, and religious factions over the future of the Yemeni state. The Yemeni republic founded in 1962 has disintegrated since 2011 as the unifying fabric of society came apart at the seams. The country stands at a historical crossroads to determine the underlying question of what it currently means to be a citizen of Yemen.

1

REGIONS, SECTS, AND TRIBES

I beg you, my pen, to feel and experience:
  Will the world quake and shudder while we stay sleeping?
Arise, my pen, and call to your nation:
  It is time for you to speak to your people.
You've set your poetry ablaze around them for so long now,
  A roaring bonfire of meters and rhymes.
When you kindle it with your breath, you blow away their sleep
  Yet the dreams under their eyelids laugh at you.
You shouted in their ears and they moved,
  But alas, they merely stirred in their slumber.
We fear the tyrant's sword, yet its edge is blunt.
  We worship idols, yet they are mere rubble.
Our entire nation is subject to the whims of a single person;
  Not even sheep follow along so blindly!
We made him a gift of our bodies and belongings,
  And yet he only sees vile treason wherever he looks.
We built a throne for him to sit as its sovereign, but built
  A prison instead, in whose shadow we are scorned and abused.
Our heads bow low to him in submission
  And our feet can barely move for the burden of their shackles. As
often as our tongues invoke him in prayer, so too
  do they taste his draught of sudden death.
How many fathers have offered their lives to the Imām,
  Who then let their orphans die of hunger.
  He siphons off the riches of his people and lets them die

In hunger in order to fatten the cult of his eminence.
His vituperations are sacred; verily they are blessings,
  Miracles, and judgements brought from on high.
In his view, the labor of mankind is heresy and he'll take
  No part in it; yet he calls himself Law and Order.

—Muhammad al-Zubayri (1910–1965),
"A Call to the Sleepers"[1]

What religion is practiced in Yemen?

On the prophet Muhammad's passing, one group of early Muslims elected Abu Bakr, a companion of the prophet, to be the first caliph or leader of the Islamic community, which centuries later became known as Sunni Islam, meaning the followers of the *sunna*, or "tradition." This group of Muslims and later generations of caliphs were opposed to religious leadership succession based on Muhammad's bloodline. The Sunni sect of Islam consists of four historic schools of *madhab*, or "legal thought": Maliki, Hanafi, Hanbali, and Shafi'i. Of the four, Hanbali is the most religiously conservative branch and is the dominant jurisprudence of Saudi Arabia and the Wahabi sect of Islam. The Shafi'i school of thought, named after the jurist Muhammad ibn Idris al-Shafi'i, is the most prevalent religious sect in Yemen and can also be found in Southeast Asia, South Asia, the Levant, and Egypt. Under 16th-century Ottoman rule, and again in the 19th century, Shafi'i adherents expanded their numbers and territory in the southern and western regions of Yemen, as well as in the eastern regions of Hadramawt.

In opposition to Abu Bakr was another group of Muslims who instead supported the succession of Ali, Muhammad's cousin and son-in-law, going on to form an alternate Islamic sect of Shi'i Islam, stemming from the term *shi'atu Ali*, or "partisans of Ali." When Ali's son Hussein was killed by opponents during a historic revolt in Karbala in 680 BCE, he became a martyr and a symbol of the oppressed, sanctifying the family's bloodline as a mark of religious leadership. The Shi'i communities of the Persian Gulf and Iran commemorate the day with a bloody self-flagellation ceremony. Shi'i

---

1. Muḥammad Maḥmūd al-Zubayrī, *Ṣalāh fī al-jaḥīm*. Sana'a: Dār al-Kalima, 1985. Translated by Sam Liebhaber, 59–66.

Islam is itself divided into subsects that base their theology on different ancestral lineage. Zaydi Islam, practiced primarily in Yemen, diverged from the mainstream Shi'a sect during the time of their fifth imam named Zayd bin Ali, the great-grandson of the Prophet Muhammad's son-in-law Ali. In the 9th century CE, Yahya bin Hussein al-Hadi (859–911 CE), a prominent religious scholar from the city of Madinah, brought Shi'i Islam to the highlands of Yemen, where it has remained dominant ever since. The followers of Zaydi Islam exercise religious hegemony over the northern highlands of Yemen where they constitute the large majority of the region's population.

The Zaydi branch was founded on the principle that imamic, or religious leadership, succession should not be based on heredity and dynastic rule, but rather that the leadership should be chosen by an elected group of *ulema* (scholars) and *sadah* (descendants of the Prophet Muhammad) on the basis of fourteen qualities including religious piety, knowledge, and valor. Imams were subject to public scrutiny and were liable to be removed from office in instances of corruption or incompetence. It was not until the 1920s when Imam Yahya anointed his son Ahmad as his successor that the Zaydi tradition was broken, leading to growing opposition to Yahya's Hamid al-Din family and culminating in the 1962 revolution.

The Shafi'i-Zaydi divide between North and South Yemen is more a reflection of regional topographic differences between highland, lowland, and coastal regions than religious sectarianism. Zaydis live primarily in the highlands between Sana'a and Sa'dah, while the Shafi'is live in the coastal, southern, and eastern regions of the country. There are several doctrinal differences between the two groups, primarily in how leadership is chosen. Zaydis have historically been ruled by an imam, following the Shi'i traditions of Hassan and Hussein. Shafi'is, on the other hand, do not prioritize religious or spiritual qualifications in selecting their leadership, relying instead on local political rulers known as sultans. In actuality, Shafi'i and Zaydi Islam share a similar *fiqh*, or jurisprudence, and Zaydis have traditionally maintained a limited reverence for the original caliphs of Sunni Islamic history. These similarities are even more pronounced in Yemen, where both religious groups prioritize oral education and memorized recitations and frequently attend prayer services in either denomination's mosque.

Aside from Zaydis and Shafi'is, there is also a significant minority of Yemeni Ismailis, another sect of Shi'i Islam. The Ismailis split from Zaydi followers around the time of the fifth imam, as Ismailis recognized Muhammad al-Baqir as the successor imam rather than Zayd bin Ali. The term "Ismaili" derives from their sect's recognition of al-Baqir's eldest grandson as the seventh imam rather than his younger brother Musa al-Kazim. In a simplistic delineation of Shi'i sects, Zaydis are called "fivers" because they revere Zayd bin Ali as the fifth and final imam; Ismailis as "seveners" for their belief that Ismail was the seventh and final imam, thus granting his name to their sect; and finally Iranian Shi'is, or Jaafari, are "twelvers" because their tradition continued the imamic dynasty through the descendants of Musa al-Kazim to the 12th imam who disappeared and will return as *Mahdi* or "the guided one," an Islamic version of the redeemer. Ismaili communities number around 200,000 and currently reside in the Haraz and Ibb regions of central Yemen in addition to Najran, a region that sits along the disputed northern border between Saudi Arabia and Yemen. Ismailism in Yemen is famously associated with the 11th-century reign of Queen Arwa over the Sulayhid state, breaking the taboo of female leadership in Yemen. A mosque was built in her name that can still be visited in the central Yemeni town of Jibla.

There is also a minority of Yemeni Sufis, a sect most closely associated with mystical practices and ancestor reverence. The most recognizable Sufi practice is the annual tomb visitations to the shrine of specific Yemeni saints or scholars, a ritual deemed by many Zaydis to be idolatrous. The largest Yemeni Sufi orders are located in South Yemen and the eastern Hadramawt region, which has exercised a historic impact on religion across the Indian Ocean. When Hadrami merchants first emigrated to South and Southeast Asia and proselytized Islam during the 13th century, they brought with them the values and practices of Sufi Islam, despite the fact that the sect remains a minority within the nation of Islam. The Hadrami city of Tarim, considered by Sufis as the sect's spiritual capital in Yemen, is also the site of Dar al-Mustafa, a new Sufi school founded by Sufi scholar Habib Umar, which has been at the center of the sect's religious revival since 2000. Sufi expansion and shrine pilgrimages continue to be a point of contention between the sects, especially as groups of Salafis have frequently sought to destroy these tombs and shrines in religious retribution.

Is there a history of sectarian violence in Yemen?

There is a long history of religious tolerance and respect between Zaydi and Shafi'i populations. Tribal tensions, particularly among members of Hashid and Bakil, the two large tribal federations that inhabit the majority of the northern highlands, were limited to disputes over natural resources and familial conflicts rather than religious doctrine. Absence of sectarian violence did not mean that there were no doctrinal disputes or divergent religious opinions, but it did mean that religion was not an inherent source of conflict. In recent decades, as Saudi proselytizing has encroached into Yemeni society, these tensions have flared up and manifested themselves in the Houthi uprising.

The spread of Salafis in Yemen and across the Middle East over the past five decades has had a destabilizing effect on political and social life. Vocal and radical voices within the Salafi movement have advocated violence, terrorism, and political upheaval in an effort to restore Islam to what some Salafis consider its former glory. Not all Salafis share these beliefs, however. A growing number of "quietist Salafis" have eschewed political activism and publicly declared their opposition to revolutions. Within Yemen, these quietist Salafis often cite two ominous Middle Eastern historical examples of the unintended consequences of political revolution: deposing Egyptian King Farouk in 1952 brought about the secularist regime of Gamal Abdel Nasser and the anti-colonial war against Britain in South Yemen that produced the Arab World's first and only communist regime. The conservative critique that overthrowing a monarchy only succeeds in spawning an emperor has guided the decisions made by this ultra-conservative Salafi group in Yemen since the 1980s and has largely discouraged the group from political confrontation. The movement's de facto leader, Muqbil Bin Hadi al-Wadi'i, founded Dar al-Hadith, a house of religious learning in the village of Dammaj near the northern city of Sa'dah. The Dammaj school was at the center of a nationwide organization of religious learning centers, bookstores, and a growing membership.

Until his death from liver cancer in July 2001, al-Wadi'i steered his movement away from direct opposition to Ali Abdullah Saleh and the Yemen Arab Republic (YAR). His apolitical stance, however, did not dissuade him from confronting the Zaydi scholars and teaching centers that dominated northern religious life. Al-Wadi'i spent many years studying in Saudi Arabia before being expelled from the country after authorities suspected his involvement in an attack on the Grand Mosque of Mecca in 1979. After founding his school in Dammaj, al-Wadi'i developed a following across the Middle East and North Africa through his many publications and recorded sermons. Soon large numbers of students began to arrive in Dammaj, and there were 1,000 participants by the end of the 1990s. Many enrollees in the Dammaj school and the largest proponents of Salafi Islam were Yemeni migrant workers who returned from employment abroad having been indoctrinated by Saudi Wahabi preachers. At the Dammaj school, students focused on Islamic law, theology, and *hadith*, or the sayings of the Prophet Muhammad, and upon graduation carried their mentor's message to other institutes and mosques throughout Yemen. Religious doctrine was spread not only through peaceful education but also through violence that was encouraged and supported by Saleh's government. In 1994, Salafis were called upon to dismantle the last remnants of the Yemen Socialist Party in South Yemen. In addition to targeting socialists, Salafis destroyed Sufi shrines and even leveled the Seera brewery owned by the National Brewing Company in Aden, the only legal brewery in the Arabian Peninsula.

What is a tribe and what role does it play in Yemeni society?

For centuries, *qaba'el*, or tribes, in Yemen have been the most prominent wielders of economic, political, and social power in South Arabia. Aside from a small minority of nomadic Bedouin tribes in Yemen's eastern Hadramawt regions, the country's tribes are largely sedentary, having centuries earlier settled down to a primarily agricultural existence. Tribes in Yemen are united behind a common identity as the descendants of their ancient ancestor Qahtan. Within these mythical origins are individual tribal identities often united by a shared distant ancestor or by a specified territorial boundary. Next to immediate family and religious piety, tribal affiliation is the most important marker of a Yemeni. Allegiance to a central state, when one did exist, was and continues to be only a comparatively distant notion.

Communal life is dictated by *urf*, or a code of tribal law based on tradition and religious customs. Personal conduct is guided by a sense of *sharaf*, or honor, centered around family, marriage, and the equitable resolution of disputes. It is this tribal conflict resolution that often garners the most public attention, as does the image of a tribesman waving a ceremonial dagger above his head. Episodes of violence, revenge, and the murder of a promiscuous daughter are not infrequent. Tribesmen have long taken pride in their weapons, earning a reputation as some of the best marksmen in the region. Ownership of arms and the ability to recruit thousands of able-bodied militiamen at short notice is an essential part of tribal power politics. The *jambiyya*, or curved ceremonial dagger, is also a status symbol based on the quality, design, and jewels found on its hilt. Jews and other social inferiors were barred from carrying weapons in public. Once made by Jewish silversmiths, jambiyyas, a fixture of Yemeni tribal culture, are now being imported from China as the artisan community famous for their production was never replaced after the Jewish exodus in 1949.

As ubiquitous as weapons may be in Yemen, minor conflicts do not always become violent. Well-respected judicial traditions, local *qadis* or religious judges, and tribal councils often resolve disputes before resorting to arms. Even during the first civil war in the 1960s, the principal tribes met semi-annually to discuss the larger question of foreign intervention, to issue a series of legislative decrees, and to express a sincere interest in bringing the conflict to a peaceful resolution. Rather than be defined by violence and fighting, tribal life is a rich cultural experience. Communal dances, poetry recitations, religious education, and the elaborate celebrations of life milestones and holidays are important parts of idyllic tribal life and manifestations of Yemen's rich cultural and social history.

What is a tribal confederation and how much influence does it have in Yemen?

The interests of individual tribes do not preclude cooperation and allegiance to neighboring tribes. Since the collapse of the Sabean Kingdom in the 3rd century CE, Yemeni tribes have coalesced into tribal alliances called confederations. In contemporary Yemen, the only two remaining tribal confederations are the Hashid (north and west of Sana'a) and Bakil (north and east of Sana'a). These two confederations are united by a mutual defense pact and are guided by a council of tribal sheikhs who are responsible both for adjudicating disputes and mobilizing tribesmen for war. According to tribal urf, each tribe is held responsible for the conduct of its tribesmen and must respond to the onset of a feud either through a judicial ruling to the satisfaction of both parties or through force of arms. Similar to the biblical concept of a city of refuge, the Zaydi imams created tribal settlements known as *hijrahs*, or sanctuary cities, where violence was banned and where warring parties could enter arbitration and reach an amenable compromise. Hijrahs continue to be sources of religious education and a key to preserving law and order in the tribal hinterland, away from the influence of encroaching political institutions.

Since the formation of the republican state, tribes have become more heavily involved in the country's politics. Tribal sheikhs have dominated the early National Assembly (1969); its successor, the Consultative Council (1971); and the contemporary political parties and military leadership. The power of the Hashid and Bakil confederations is such that no central body has managed to fully control their territory and political life. Aside from the short-lived presidency of Ibrahim al-Hamdi (1974–1977), no Yemeni leader has successfully confronted the tribal domination of the Yemeni state. The phrase "dancing on the head of snakes" has often been attributed to former Yemeni president Ali Abdullah Saleh, not in respect of his coercion of the tribes but rather for his ability to play off tribal leaders against each other and avoid the poisonous venom of any number of conflicts or sheikhs that could have toppled his three decades of presidency. In December 2017, Saleh missed a dance step and overplayed his hand against the Houthis, leading to his assassination in the streets of Sana'a by the very tribes he sought to cajole.

Since the 1960s, Yemeni nationalism has endeavored to foster a homogenous Yemeni identity by creating a notion of citizenry apart from loyalty to an individual tribe or tribal alliance. In recognition of the importance of the tribe as a concept in South Arabian society, republican leaders have transformed the state itself into an all-encompassing tribe. Ali Abdullah Saleh used tribal rhetoric in his orations in an effort to depict the notion of "Yemeni" as synonymous with tribesmen, thus idealizing the mythos of the *qabili*, or tribal warrior. Accordingly, the state itself constitutes one large tribal umbrella that encompasses the entire population. Equating the state and the tribe, Shaykh 'Abdullah al-Ahmar, the former speaker of parliament and head of the Hashid Federation, considered himself the guardian of the state, an entity united by its common tribal identity, which transcends all but Islam.

Does Yemen have distinct regions or is the entire country homogenous?

Prior to the unification of North and South Yemen in 1990, there was never a single Yemeni state that covered the geographic borders of the current state of Yemen. There are five distinct regions, unique in their culture, local dialect, climate, economy, and modern political formation: Hadramawt, Aden, northern Yemen, middle Yemen, and the Tihama (see Map 1).

Hadramawt, which literally means "death has come," is the country's largest desert region, located in the easternmost section of Yemen, with population centers limited to the areas around Wadi Hadramawt, a watercourse and subsidiary sources of groundwater. The region's relative stability is due to its uninhabitable desert boundaries to the north and south. Hadramawt's culture and people are distinct from the rest of Yemen, with many families maintaining commercial and familial connection across the Indian Ocean with expatriate Hadrami communities.

Aden and its hinterland, centered around the city's port, oil refinery, and urban population, are the political and economic center of South Yemen. Abyan province, located northeast of Aden, was used by the British colonial administration as the port's breadbasket. Recently, Abyan has garnered public attention as the home of al-Qaeda's leaders, including Jalal Baledi al-Marqashi and Nasir al-Wuhayshi. Yemeni president Mansur Hadi is from Abyan, which may help to explain his aggressive anti–al-Qaeda strategy in his home province.

Northern Yemen, whose highlands are some of the most rugged mountainous terrain in the world, is also the tribal base for the Houthi movement and historically constituted the great majority of

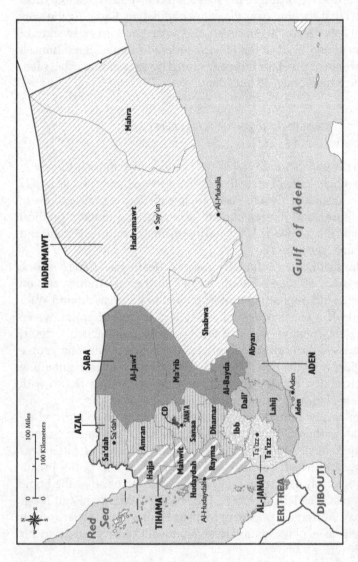

Map 1 Yemen Regional Map

the imam's tribal allies. Northern Yemen can be divided into Hajjah, Sa'dah, and al-Jawf. Hajjah is the provincial capital of Yemen's northwest region, traditionally the refuge and northern stronghold of the Zaydi imamate and the site of an infamous prison for the imam's most dangerous opponents. Sa'dah is the northernmost province and city in Yemen, best known for its strong religious identification with Zaydi Islam and home to the graves of the imamate's founders. It is dominated by a frontier mentality and has long been a haven for smugglers across the Saudi border. Al-Jawf is a large geographic region northeast of Sana'a that stretches from the town of Amran to the Saudi border. Al-Jawf only came under direct government control during the 1980s, and while it remains semi-autonomous it has recently served as a haven for Islamist groups crossing the Saudi border, attracting increased international intervention.

Middle Yemen includes most of the country's population, paved roads, and economic opportunity. The capital city of Sana'a and the surrounding mountains are home to millions of Yemenis from all parts of the country looking for employment, education, or political favor. To the east of Sana'a lies the city of Marib, which was sparsely populated for most of Yemen's modern history. It is known primarily for the ancient sites of the Marib dam and the capital of the Sabean Kingdom. The discovery of oil and natural gas in the Marib basin during the 1980s has increased the wealth and importance of the local region. During the 2014 conflict, the relative stability in Marib has attracted a continuous flow of internally displaced refugees and their families, significantly increasing the size of the local population. Marib has emerged as an island of stability amid the violence and uncertainty of the current Houthi war.

To the south of Sana'a, Ibb province and the city of Ta'iz, the country's agricultural and commercial capital, are the main centers of Shafi'i population in North Yemen. To the southeast of Sana'a is al-Baydah, which divides the Abyan region from the desert highlands. It was previously the easternmost province of North Yemen and had a long tradition of north-south smuggling and border skirmishes. In February 2017, Al-Baydah was the scene of some of the most intense fighting between Houthis and al-Qaeda, with US commandos intervening in the small village of Yakla.

The Tihama region is a long narrow coastline along Yemen's western frontier abutting the Red Sea as far south as Bab al-Mandeb.

Its terrain and climate are particularly harsh, hot and humid, as it is one of the few regions of Yemen at sea level. The people of Tihama have long been subservient to those in the highlands, although the region's sparse population resides in the vicinity of the country's greatest untapped sources of water. The Tihama Development Authority has demonstrated a degree of organizational continuity since the 1970s, a stark exception to the lack of government oversight in the rest of the country. The region's Hodeidah port has grown in importance since the 1960s and is currently a main transit point for international economic and humanitarian aid. Zabid, a major inland town in Tihama is best known as a center of ancient learning and has been declared a world heritage site by UNESCO. Located about halfway between Hodeidah and Tihama's second port of Mokha, Zabid's utilization of scarce water resources serves as a model for other Wadi development projects.

The varying Yemeni terrain, which includes coastal flatlands, rough mountains, and vast deserts, creates natural impediments to the free flow of population and goods. Yemen's population of 29 million is disperse, spread out among 135,000 villages and settlements, some built into mountainsides, others found along isolated desert wadis. Only one-third of Yemenis live in urban areas, making it far more difficult for the central government in Sana'a to exercise authority and administer basic social services. As a result, many subregions within Yemen exist semi-autonomously, providing their own health care, schools, and public services and maintaining local roads and infrastructure.

Who are the Hadramis?

As a starting point, it might be pertinent to ask first how a Yemeni became the governor of Jakarta, Indonesia, in 2017. Anies Baswedan, a public intellectual, prominent Indonesian politician, and current governor of Jakarta, is a distant descendant of Hadrami migrants to Indonesia and still carries the Hadrami last name, indicated by the "Ba" preceding his family name. His grandfather, Abdurrahman Baswedan, was an Indonesian freedom fighter and one of the country's earliest and most prominent politicians. Hundreds of years earlier, Yemenis living in the eastern region of Hadramawt established commercial networks across the Indian Ocean, thriving as a diasporic merchant community. In the 21st century, Hadrami communities can be found in the Horn of Africa, down the eastern African coast, and along the Indian Ocean basin. Despite, in some cases, hundreds of years separating these communities from their initial emigration from Yemen, Hadramis continue to identify with their country of origin and take an active interest in its politics and economy.

Hadramawt, Yemen's eastern desert region, is home to 1.2 million people who constitute about 5.2% of Yemen's population, although the area represents more than half of Yemen's territory at 193,000 square kilometers. The Hadramawt Governorate has substantial hydrocarbon reserves and produces a native honey considered by connoisseurs to be one of the finest in the world. Hadramawt is famous for its role at the center of the ancient spice trade centered around the historic cities of Shibam, Tarim, and Say'un. This culture of entrepreneurship has come to define Hadramis and their region. Since the arrival of Islam at the end of the 7th century, Hadramis have become a population of economic migrants to the growing urban regions of northern Yemen, to the Arabian Peninsula, and across the Indian Ocean. Emigration was both an escape from the harsh regional climate and a path toward economic prosperity for the emigré whose extended family remained behind in Hadramawt.

The Hadrami diaspora, numbering close to 12 million, has risen to economic, political, and social prominence in east Africa, India, Indonesia, and nearly every country in the Indian Ocean region. Hadramis established mercantile communities overseas, bringing with them a unique version of Islam and constituting the religious seed of some of the world's largest Muslim populations. The two ports of Shihr and Mukalla served as departure points for a growing number of Hadramis who sought to escape the poverty, drought, and political instability of southern Arabia to seek their fortunes abroad. Remittances and waqf development projects funded by the Hadrami diaspora have supported Hadrami civil society and infrastructure in the absence of similar support by the central Yemeni state. Of particular note is the large number of Hadrami migrants who were welcomed into Saudi Arabia during the 1970s and 1980s and who rose to prominence in the construction and commercial sectors, like the Bin Laden family. Saúdis have traditionally exercised a much more lenient employment and immigration policy toward Hadramis than to other Yemenis.

The region's unique history and identity, its wealthy diasporic community, a plethora of natural resources, remote geography, and a relatively large percentage of highly educated individuals has created a sense of "Hadrami exceptionalism" as a distinct identity and social group distinct from the rest of Yemen. Hadramis have long valued their autonomy and are reluctant to come, once again, under the aegis of a central government either in Sana'a or Aden. In an attempt to appeal to Hadramis for support, Mansur Hadi added the neighboring regions of Shabwa and Mahra to the Hadramawt Governorate as part of a 2015 Six Region plan for Yemen, a political move that only served to further inflame tensions surrounding regional identities.

Where does Hadramawt fit into the modern history of Yemen?

Hadramis have always sought a degree of independence and autonomy from the western regions of Yemen and the various republican governments that have ruled Yemen since 1962. Under the British, Hadramawt was known as the East Aden Protectorate, which included the northern desert region—the Empty Quarter. After the British withdrawal in 1967, Hadramawt joined the People's Democratic Republic of Yemen (PDRY) in the south. The unity was forced on Hadramawt by President Qahtan al-Sha'abi, who crushed the nascent People's Democratic Republic of Hadramawt, enforcing Aden's suzerainty over the region. Although several Hadramis rose to political prominence in the PDRY, such as Ali Salem al-Beidh and Haydar al-Attas, Hadramawt scarcely benefited from South Yemen's relations with the Soviet Union. Tens of thousands of Hadramis fled the incessant political unrest and repression in the PDRY during the 1970s and 1980s, choosing instead to join Hadrami communities abroad. The brutality of the PDRY years has made a generation of Hadramis suspicious of associating once again with a southern separatist movement, fearing dominance by the Abyan leadership. A minority of Hadramis, especially those involved in the PDRY before the 1986 civil war, remain optimistic about the future of an independent South Yemen state with Hadramawt as a prominent component.

After 1990, Hadramawt became part of the united Republic of Yemen (ROY). Ali Abdullah Saleh took control of the region and pushed Hadrami leaders to the periphery of Yemeni politics. Hadrami leadership had been split over the decision to join the ROY, with Ali Salim al-Beidh emerging as the leading voice to join the ROY in what he assumed would be a federal state. During the 1994 civil war, al-Beidh led a coalition of Hadramis in his disillusioned opposition to Saleh's original 1990 power-sharing agreements. In the aftermath of the civil war, Hadramawt had lost an even greater degree of its political voice in the ROY. Saleh took advantage of Hadrami weakness and fully exploited new oil discoveries in the Masila basin, funding his personal patronage network rather than investing in Hadramawt's infrastructure. An exception to Hadrami political irrelevance occurred in 2006 when the Joint Meeting Party (JMP) selected a Hadrami, Faisal bin Shamlan, to run against Saleh in the presidential elections, which Saleh unsurprisingly won handily. Faraj bin Ghanem, another prominent Hadrami, resigned his post as prime minister in opposition to Saleh's conduct of the election and other issues of political corruption.

As the former Yemen Socialist Party (YSP) began to lose a political following, its earlier leaders, al-Beidh, al-Attas, and Hassan Baum, formed the al-Hirak southern separatist movement as a southern nationalist opposition to Saleh's northern regime. The movement started as a campaign of civil disobedience centered around the southern port city of Mukalla, which accomplished little else other than to weaken the social fabric and to open up the region to the growing presence of al-Qaeda in Mukalla.

Although the population surrounding Wadi Hadramawt is the most populous representative of the eastern regions, it is not the only political voice nor the only area of domestic and international interest. For instance, al-Mahra, the easternmost governorate of Hadramawt, which borders both Oman and Saudi Arabia, is one of the country's most sparsely population regions, yet has become a center for smuggling drugs and weapons, thus making it a particular area of security interest for regional powers. The governorate had been coerced into the newly created South Yemen state in 1967, an affront to its long history of independence and the unique culture and identity of its residents. Similarly, Mahris have protested the growing presence of Saudi Arabia since 2017, with many fearing the loss of autonomy to foreign intervention.

The extreme poverty and lack of modern infrastructure such as running water, electricity, and cellphones has not dampened the sense of local autonomy in al-Mahra, a sentiment strengthened by recent grassroots movements. These movements, including the Mahra Youth United Association, organized relatively large protests in the governorate's capital of al-Ghayda against the proposed federalization of Yemen, a decision that would again make al-Mahra subservient to the more populated and wealthy regions of Hadramawt. The al-Mahra model of local governance and grassroots civil society development has stemmed the tide of al-Qaeda expansion across the rest of Yemen's southern and eastern regions. Without constructive international attention and investment, the Mahris and the lucrative smuggling and black market in their territory will fall into the hands of al-Qaeda affiliates, potentially endangering important border regions.

2

ARABIA FELIX—AN EARLY
HISTORY OF YEMEN

In the time of Sam ibn Nuh,
Sana'a was ancient castles
    and silver windows.
A dove traced her form after the tidal wave receded
    and the flood grew quiet.
The dove circles over her minarets
and sings to its ancestors
the song of candles that flicker at dusk
    dancing over the hills,
the ancient songs that glide, glittering in the streets.
The houses are warmed and wrapped in incense,
Courtyards are infused with gentle words:
"Sana'a sleeps under the Throne of God
and anoints her tree blossoming with perfume."[1]
    — Abd al-Aziz al-Maqalih (1937–), "The Third Qasidah"

What is the earliest recorded history of settlement in Yemen?

What is the connection between the biblical story of Noah's flood
and Yemen? The answer to this question can tell us a great deal
about how ancient chroniclers and modern-day Yemenis view their
own country. According to local tradition, Noah's son Shem exited

---

1. 'Abd Al-'Azīz Maqālih, Bob Holman, and Sam Liebhaber. *The Book of Sana'a: Poetry of 'Abd Al-'Azīz Al-Maqālih.* Yemen Translation Series (Ardmore, PA: American Institute for Yemeni Studies, 2004), 36–39.

the ark after the flood in search of a place to live and came across the fertile lands of South Arabia. It is here that Noah built Sana'a, which tradition claims to have been the world's first city. South Arabian ancestry is similarly traced through Qahtan, the great-great-grandson of Shem. This traditional Arab genealogy is often referenced in poetry, history books, and contemporary political speeches when the peoples of Yemen are referred to in a unifying and cohesive manner as "the sons of Qahtan."

The Queen of Sheba is one the earliest and best-known figures of ancient pre-Christian Yemen, although Ethiopians do maintain a tradition associating the Horn of Africa with the Kingdom of Sheba as well. The Sabean capital of Marib and the ancient remnants of the 2,500-year-old Marib Dam are among the most famous archeological sites in Arabia and are a testament to the wealth and importance of South Arabia in the ancient regional spice trade. Known in modern Yemen as Mahram Bilquis, or Bilquis' Sanctuary, the Sabean-era Awam Temple is the largest pre-Islamic Arabian structure and the site of multiple excavations since the 1950s. In a time before the extravagance of the Saudi oil sheikhs, the spice merchants were the barons of Arabia. The Sabean Kingdom of South Arabia exported 3,000 tons of incense and 600 tons of myrrh annually, receiving vast sums of silver from Levantine and European consumers.

Ancient Egyptians, Greeks, and Romans all coveted the land's wealth of frankincense and myrrh and tried unsuccessfully to exercise dominion over local tribal Arabs. This marked the beginning of centuries of imperial rivalry over South Arabia as one power after another sought to gain control over the spice trade and maritime ports. No external dominion was long in duration as the mountains of northern Yemen were an impervious obstacle to large-scale invasions, thus limiting occupations to the country's coastal regions.

Although you can still purchase these spices in Yemen, when was the last time that your local supermarket carried frankincense and myrrh? The emergence of Christianity and advancements in shipping technology led to a decline in the spice trade and in South Arabia's overall economic fortunes. While Roman temples burned incense as a daily ritual, early church leaders banned the practice as they deemed it to be a pagan practice. By the 1st century CE, Roman ship construction and navigation facilitated easier transport along the Red Sea rather than via the camel caravans of Arabia.

Archeological evidence is not all that remains from this heyday of South Arabia. The terrace farming along the mountainous northern regions together with irrigation tunnels dug through the rocky sides of the mountain remain the bedrock of Yemeni farming and a visual staple of the countryside. The roads that once connected a famous spice region to the world are the same roads that connect Yemen's modern-day cities, although some have since been paved.

The South Arabian Sabean Kingdom was conquered by an equally famous monarchy known as the Himyarate Kingdom (110 BCE–525 CE). One of the most memorable historical episodes of the Himyars was their conversion to Judaism around 380 CE and the abandonment of a polytheistic and pagan culture. The Jewish Kingdom lasted less than 150 years before it was overthrown by an Ethiopian Kingdom that had converted to Christianity. Despite questions as to the sincerity of the conversion and as to what extent the Himyar Kings practiced traditional Judaism, the very existence of a pre-modern Jewish Kingdom in Arabia continues to excite the stories of myth rivaled only by stories of King Solomon and the Queen of Sheba.

What does the name "Yemen" mean and why is Yemen called "Arabia Felix"?

The self-proclaimed centrality of Yemen to the history of the world and to Islam specifically is further espoused in the local belief that the name Yemen is a description of the country's position relative to Mecca and Medina—*yamin*, meaning to the right in Arabic. While these beliefs pervade notions of common national and cultural identity, the country's name most likely refers to its southern location on the Arabian Peninsula—*al-Yaman* or "the south." The city of Sana'a began as a roadside outpost in biblical times before gradually growing into a city, taking advantage of its position along the spice route centered in the ancient Sheba capital of Marib.

Arabia Felix, or Happy Arabia, dates to Greco-Roman times and was an expression of pleasant surprise at discovering the highlands of Yemen in South Arabia. After long treks through some of the most arid regions of the world, Yemen's green mountainsides and wealthy ancient cultures must have truly seemed like the mythological Elysian Fields.

What is unique about Yemen's geography and climate?

In a part of the world known for its expansive deserts, Yemen's topography is surprisingly varied with mountain ranges, coastal plains, lush fields, and islands featuring unique fauna and species. To be sure, half the country is desert. Known as Rubh al-Khali, or the Empty Quarter, these deserts in the eastern half of the country stretched over 250,966 square miles, connecting Yemen with the expansive Arabian deserts of Saudi Arabia and Oman.

Geographic determinism has placed Yemen at the meeting point of the Indian and Red Seas, at the center of international commerce over millennia, and within the fortuitous range of the Asian monsoon rains. During the rainy season from April through August, the Yemeni highlands receive an average of 47 inches of rain, which is more precipitation than falls in Seattle, Washington, where residents spend more than 150 days a year sitting under an umbrella.

While there are no natural lakes or rivers in Yemen, there are seasonal bodies of water that carry torrents of rain down the mountainside to the dry coastal regions and irrigating fields along its path. These flash floods, which can certainly be destructive in the short term, are also the lifeline of Yemen's agricultural economy. One of the most captivating sights in Yemen are the mountainside terraces, with stone walls constructed to capture runoff and sediment after each rainstorm and in the process develop additional arable land along the sides of the country's mountainous terrain. Farther down the mountains and toward the coasts, farmers have developed a centuries-old method of spate irrigation, which diverts the wadi waters to flood-irrigate nearby fields through the digging of small tributary canals. The area between Sana'a and Aden, known as Middle Yemen, and the fields surrounding the western port city of Hodeida in particular, continue to be the country's breadbasket and the source of valuable crops for domestic consumption and export. Despite an elaborate system of rainwater utilization, crop yields continue to depend on rainfall and on the use of limited groundwater. Yemen's current population has outgrown its water resources, leading to a situation where a growing number of households, even in a major city like Ta'iz, need to have water delivered by truck on a regular basis and stored in makeshift cisterns.

How important was the port of Aden in Yemen's history?

Bab al-Mandab, the entrance to the Red Sea in the southwest corner of the country, is one of the most important waterways in the world. Even before the opening of the Suez Canal in 1869, the gates of the Red Sea were a vital transit point connecting the Asian spice trade with Europe. The peninsula of Aden, located 100 miles east of Bab al-Mandab, thus served as an important transshipment and resupply port during the Middle Ages and again after the British seized the city in 1839. In the interim, South Arabia was in the crossfire of imperial rivalry as the Portuguese, Ottomans, Egyptians, British, and French competed for control of this strategic position between India and Egypt. The combination of warfare, periodic sieges, the emergence of rival ports, and new shipping technology that decreased reliance on wind direction led to a decline in Aden's importance, to the extent that when the British first encountered the port in 1837, it was little more than a fishing village of several hundred residents.

The earliest mention of the port city of Aden was in the 1st century CE when Greek traders encountered a village with natural harbors that had once been an important midway station for oceanic trade between India and Egypt. Indeed, Aden and its position along the incense and spice routes was traditionally considered to be one of the 13 fabled pre-Islamic markets of Arabia. In the 9th and 10th centuries CE, Aden again became a prominent commercial center as the regional Islamic empire shifted from Iraq to Egypt under the Fatimids, thus relocating trade and prominence to the Red Sea. Aden is mentioned by the great Arab chroniclers as a major port of entrepôt and a prize in the eyes of regional powers who sought naval security and revenue from the India trade. Under the Ayyubid dynasty in the 12th century CE, Aden became a natural maritime base along the Indian Ocean and a center of trade during the Middle Ages.

Much of what we know about daily life in Aden during the Middle Ages has been gleaned from records found in Egypt's Cairo Geniza, or a special synagogue storeroom of discarded private and public letters, accounts, and miscellaneous writings. The Cairo Geniza documents, considered the world's most famous and extensive geniza collection, were found in the Ben Ezra Synagogue in the old city of Cairo. From among these 750,000 documents, the famous scholar Shlomo Dov Goitein compiled *Mediterranean Society*, a five-volume social and economic history of the Mediterranean Sea region during the Middle Ages. Similar research projects have focused specifically on Aden, providing a window into a period of history that demonstrates how this port city served as a midway point between Jewish mercantile communities in Alexandria, Europe, and India and as a cosmopolitan city that simultaneously hosted sailors from China, Ethiopia, India, and Persia. The city's physical structure, legislative system, taxation, social life, and commercial enterprises were driven by the need to maintain and facilitate the maritime trade route through Aden. The trade wealth that flowed through Aden was one of the reasons the Rasulid dynasty (1128–1454) constituted a golden era for South Arabia and a moment in time often remembered with nostalgia by Yemeni chroniclers.

There are no natural resources in Aden and the city is dependent on water from outside sources. Yet the port's strategic location at the mouth of the Red Sea has time and again made it the target of imperial ambitions. This was true in 1538 when Ottoman admiral Suleiman Pasha seized the city with the intention of using Aden as a naval base for operations against the Portuguese Empire on the Indian Ocean. As it turned out, Aden was not the garrison city that the Ottomans hoped it would be. Local Adeni residents killed the garrisoned Ottoman soldiers and invited the Portuguese to assume control of the city, bringing with them a wealthy trade network that lasted until 1551 when an Ottoman fleet retook control of the city.

The Ottoman occupation was not limited to Aden but spread northward to capture Sana'a and subject the entire country to Ottoman suzerainty. Yemeni disdain for Ottoman control was driven both by the brutality of local rule and by religious tensions between the Zaydi Imamate and the Sunni Ottoman Sultan. These tensions reached their pinnacle in 1595 when Yemeni imam al-Qasim ibn Muhammad staged a rebellion and forced Sultan Murad IV to withdraw from Yemen entirely by 1635. A succession of Zaydi imams managed to extend their local authority over Aden and other southern areas but were gradually pushed back by the emergence of independent southern sultanates. By the end of the 18th century, "Yemen" came to connote only the northern mountainous region under Zaydi Imamate control, while the south was broken up into small autonomous sultanates. When the British first encountered South Arabia in the early 19th century, they perceived a weak and divided region surrounding a strategic port that was only a skeleton of its once-gloried self.

Who were the first travelers to encounter Yemen and record their travelogue?

There is a popular joke said about Yemen that during the 1990s there were so many anthropologists in the country that the government passed a law placing a limit of only one anthropologist per village. While this same remark has been attributed to multiple countries (perhaps a testament to the growing field of anthropology), Yemen, in particular, has exuded an aura of exotic mystery for explorers and academics for centuries. While many travelers were drawn to Yemen by its rich history and culture, others were financed by business and imperial interests, seeking to gain a better understanding of South Arabia.

The first modern chroniclers of Yemen were two of the most famous Arab explorers: Ibn al-Mujawir (13th century) and Ibn Batuta (1328). Theirs were the first preserved travelogues following Herodotus's accounts of Arabia (5th century BCE) and the reconnaissance of Alexander the Great's admiral Nearchus along the Arabian coast (4th century BCE). During the Greek and Hellenistic eras, South Arabia was an important part of numerous scientific studies including those by Aristotle's pupil Greek naturalist Theophrastus (3rd century BCE) and Eratosthenes of Cyrene, director of Alexandria's library (2nd century BCE). Early studies of South Arabia and the increasing importance of incense trade to Europe convinced Roman emperor Augustus of the potential benefit in seizing this lucrative spice trade. At Augustus's order, Aelius Gallus, prefect of Egypt, marched on Arabia Felix with 10,000 men and conquered the Yemeni territories of Jawf, al-Bayda, Baraqish, and Marib. The Roman conquest of South Arabia was recorded by Strabo and Pliny the Elder, two of Rome's prominent historians. These early accounts were used collectively to inform cartographic projects, mercantile surveys, and military maps for subsequent centuries.

The first European explorers to reach Mecca and Yemen included Lodovico de Varthema, who rounded the Cape of Good Hope and published his book *Itinerario* in 1511. Varthema, the first known non-Muslim to visit the tomb of the Prophet Muhammad, shared accounts of his visits to Aden, the oasis of Lahej, Yarim, Sana'a, Ta'iz, Zabid, and Dhamar, singlehandedly bringing South Arabia to the minds of future European explorers. Verthema's visit to Aden was unintentionally prolonged for three months when he was imprisoned under suspicion that he was a spy for the Portuguese Empire. Although the Portuguese Empire dominated the seas during the 16th century, there are few accounts of Portuguese visits and business with Yemen during this period, aside from the tale of two Jesuit missionaries who were shipwrecked off the coast of Yemen in 1589 and managed to visit Sana'a, Marib, and many other historic sites. It was not until the discovery of coffee in South Arabia that financing became available and travel began anew to Yemen as adventurers searched for economic opportunity.

Carsten Niebuhr, the pioneer of modern explorations to Yemen, traveled by land and sea to Mokha, Sana'a, Jeddah, Egypt, and Oman from 1761 to 1767. He was commissioned by the King of Denmark, Fredrick V, to study Arabia's people, plants, language, and transport through the region toward Dutch India. Niebuhr contributed detailed accounts of Muslim cultural practices and minority populations (e.g., Jews and Indians) along with detailed maps and economic assessments of the region. *Travels through Arabia and Other Countries in the East*, published in 1792, marked the first modern scientific account of South Arabia and the travelogue against which all others would be judged.

Are there archeological surveys of Yemen? When were these undertaken?

Eighteenth-century surveys of commercial centers and ports gave way to 19th-century South Arabian archeology. During the 1830s, Thomas Arnaud, the imam's pharmacist, set out to document the archeological remains of the ancient Sabean Kingdom in the deserts southeast of Sana'a. Arnaud's account of his visit to the ruins of the ancient capital city of Marib were recorded in 1843 by Fulgence Fresnel, the French consul at Jeddah, constituting the first serious study of South Arabian archeology.

Arnaud was followed in 1869 by Joseph Halevy, another French archeologist who pioneered not only areas of archeology but also produced one of the first ethnographic studies of the Bedouin and Jewish communities in Yemen. Halevy was able to rely on the assistance of his Jewish co-religionists across the country and most importantly his local guide Hayyim Habshoush, who published his own travelogue recording events and observations. Halevy's discovery of six ancient cities and his diligent recording of archeological inscriptions, published in *Rapport sur une Mission Archeologique dans la Yemen*, remain a foundational text in multiple fields of study related to Yemen. Halevy was followed in 1882 by Eduard Glasser, an Austrian explorer who spent six years over three different expeditions meticulously documenting Yemen's topography. Aside from the major urban and commercial areas around Sana'a, Lahej, Ta'iz, Ibb, Yarim, and Ma'bar, Glasser ventured out into the country's inhospitable mountains and canyons, finally updating the cartographic work of the Hellenistic era.

Breakthroughs in mapping, archeology, and ethnography during the 19th century paved the way for an exponential increase in European explorers during the first half of the 20th century. In 1927, two geologists from Hamburg University, Carl Rathjens and Hermann von Wissmann, conducted one of the first organized excavations in Yemen at Huqqah, the site of an ancient temple outside of Sana'a. The Dutch explorer Daniel Van der Meulen accompanied Rathjens on the first European expedition to Hadramawt in 1931. Van der Muelen was on a diplomatic mission for the Netherlands Legation to extend Dutch influence on Imam Yahya's domain. Van der Meulen chose the Hadramawt region specifically because of its connection with communities of Hadramis in Dutch Indonesia.

While Rathjens and Van der Muelen garnered a great deal of public interest in Yemen, it was actually a group of intrepid British women who literally and figuratively put historic Yemen on the map. When Bernard Reilly and Harold Ingram, two of Britain's most accomplished colonial officers in South Arabia, succeeded in pacifying the Hadrami tribes through a series of treaties and Royal Air Force operations during the 1930s, the entire desert region of Hadramawt, home to some of Yemen's most ancient and well-known kingdoms, was opened to exploration. The intrepid traveler Freya Stark was accompanied by geologist Elinor Gardner and archeologist Gertrude

Caton Thompson on an excursion to Hadhramawt in 1938. Their reports of excavations in Yemen were groundbreaking and revealed details of the Sabean Kingdom's hydraulic engineering. The Marib dam, which had been an ill-understood marvel documented by Arnaud, Halevy, and Glasser, received new attention from Stark's team who unearthed remnants of the ancient structure. Freya Stark's journey to three principal Hadrami cities—Tarim, Say'un, and Shibam—was followed by an expedition by the equally famous Arabian explorer Harry St. John Philby who, in 1936, ventured out to the city of Shabwah, the ancient capital of the Hadrami kingdom.

Are there any modern-day archeological digs in Yemen?

The modern era of archeological surveys in Yemen was ushered in by Wendell Phillips, a wealthy American researcher who flew to Wadi Beihan via Aden in 1947. On his return to the United States, Phillips established the American Foundation for the Study of Man, which monetized Yemen's biblical connection in raising funds for a follow-up expedition. Accompanied by eminent biblical archeologist William Foxwell Albright in 1950, Phillips returned to al-Mukalla on the southern Yemeni coast with a team of 14, equipped with 12 trucks equipped for desert travel, carrying generators, radios, cameras, food, and a plethora of other supplies and luxuries. With this flashy entourage, Phillips carried out excavations in Beihan, the site of ancient Timna, and published a popular book, *Qataban and Sheba: Exploring the Ancient Kingdoms on the Biblical Spice Routes of Arabia*, in 1955, complete with photographs, maps, and descriptions that transported the reader to the ancient site in a novel way.

Other archeologists followed Phillips's lead with their own well-funded missions. For example, in 1951, Gonzague Ryckmans, a Belgian epigraphist, led an excavation of the ancient city of Najran on Yemen's northern border with Saudi Arabia. The first golden era of archeology in Yemen came to an abrupt halt in 1962 when a Yemeni republic was declared, and the country descended into a destabilizing civil war. It was not until the end of the 1970s that the Yemen Arab Republic stabilized the political situation and founded the General Organization for Antiquities and Libraries, charged with the mandate of preserving the country's archeological heritage and granting permissions to foreign researchers. By the early 1980s, the number of new excavations had reached a high of 15, with American, French, German, Italian, and Soviet teams vying for the limelight in disclosing Yemen's prehistory.

Political stability, modernized transportation, and increased availability of information on historic sites in Yemen opened up the country not only to well-financed missions but also to individual scholars and backpackers looking for adventure. One of the best-known of such travelers is Tim Mackintosh-Smith whose backpacking trip to Yemen and Soqotra during the early 1990s was driven by academic and linguistic curiosity along with a personal desire to retrace his British colonial and familial roots. A modern incarnation of Ibn Batuta, one of the first modern travelers to Yemen, Smith has since moved to Sana'a, adopted Yemen as his new home, and continued to publish popular books on his time in the country, most notably *Yemen: Travels in Dictionaryland* in 1997. Although Smith is likely the most famous 21st-century chronicler of Yemen travels, he is by no means the only one to have become enamored by the culture, history, language, and antiquity of one of the world's oldest kingdoms.

What about Yemen's unique architecture?

Mudbrick houses in the Old City of Sana'a present one of the most beautiful and distinctive pictures of Yemen. UNESCO designated Sana'a, Shibam, and Wadi Hadramawt as World Heritage Sites after Italian filmmaker Pier Paolo Pasolini drew international attention to Yemeni architecture and urban planning during the 1970s. The buildings' foundations are made of stone blocks and mud bricks that are held together with locally made cement. Reddish adobe brick walls rise several stories above the foundation, retaining heat in the winter and keeping the houses cool in the summer. In the mountainous regions, these tall buildings with thick walls and large windows are warmed by the winter sun. In the coastal lowlands of the Tihama and the southern regions, the windows have no glass and are fitted with wooden grilles and shutters, blocking the sun while permitting cool sea breezes during hot and humid weather.

Yemeni building style dates back hundreds and at times thousands of years. The materials and the manner of traditional construction are influenced by local climate and locally available resources. While some large-scale public projects have begun to use modern techniques and alternative materials in construction, many families want to use only the authentic bricks and stones and to undertake renovations by local skilled craftsmen using hand tools rather than machinery, regardless of the added time and expense involved. There is a deep sense of pride in Yemen's historic architecture, which only deepens the tragedy of the 2015 Saudi bombing raids that have imperiled many of these ancient structures.

Although the general structure and color of these houses is uniform, the traditional alabaster decorative additions are at the discretion of the owner and are a demonstration of wealth and prestige. Throughout the red adobe structure are ornate windows and designs. Some of these glass windows display the Star of David symbol, a relic of the Jewish masons and craftsmen of Yemen who constructed and repaired many of these homes prior to the 1950s.

The doorways to these houses are fortress-like wooden structures with oversized brass knockers and locks using large metal keys. Each door has a small covered window to allow residents, particularly women, to scrutinize visitors before entry. Stairwell ceilings and doorways are narrow and low, forcing one to crouch or bend over before entering the house or exiting from the roof. This structure was intended for defensive purposes while also forcing a sense of deference for the head of household by bending one's head in respect upon entering. It may also be that the average height of Yemenis for the past several centuries was far below that of modern-day Americans and Europeans. Regardless of the reason, it is always wise to watch your head when maneuvering in and out of historically styled Yemeni homes.

3

IMPERIAL YEMEN—OTTOMAN AND BRITISH EMPIRES

Today the sun rises in you, my country . . .
Yesterday the colonists here had
a wicked, defiant regime that
came pirates in the sea driven by the
ambitions of an evil imperial regime
a century ago. Our government remained
in the era of eclipses, humiliations, and harnessing the
land of the south . . .
O brothers of the Red Revolution, your feast
is worthy of pride and appreciation of the
Republic flags born
　　—Muhammad Said Jarada (1927–1991), revolutionary poet of
　　　　　　　　　　　　　　　South Yemen, "November 30"

What was the most important political entity in pre-revolutionary Yemen?

When newly crowned Saudi king Ibn Saud's emissaries visited Imam Yahya in 1933, searching for a mutual understanding regarding the boundary between Yemen and Saudi Arabia, Yahya famously responded: "Who is this Bedouin coming to challenge my family's 900-year rule?" For centuries before the encounter with Ibn Saud, Yemen's tribes had settled in the country's northern highlands, along the western coast, in the hinterland surrounding Aden, and around desert oases in the east. Invading armies and sporadic occupations prevented the local tribes from coalescing under a single central and indigenous governing authority.

The lack of a single uniting Yemeni identity did not mean that ancient Yemen did not thrive under foreign rule. Often considered the golden age of South Arabia, the Rasulid Dynasty (1229–1454 CE) extended its border to include the geographic boundaries of the modern Republic of Yemen, marking the only point in the country's history where Yemen was "united." This golden era came to an end when local Zaydi imams staged a successful rebellion and established temporary local dominance until the arrival of the Portuguese and the Ottoman Empire less than a century later. For the next five centuries until 1967, Yemen's history may have seemed like a cycle. Foreign powers, coveting the valuable spice trades and strategic ports, invaded South Arabia, only to discover the impenetrable mountains of North Yemen. Tenuous holds over territory were contested by northern tribesmen who eventually succeeded in regaining autonomy, only to be subject to different foreign powers decades later.

Adherents to Zaydi Islam placed an added degree of importance on the religious qualifications of their ruler, someone they believed should emulate the Prophet Muhammad's son-in-law Ali, and his sons al-Hassan and al-Hussein. Although the succession of imams was not hereditary, the candidate needed to be an upstanding member of Ahl al-Bayt, or people of the house, referring to the descendants of the Prophet Muhammad. The imam assumed the title of *amir al-mu'minin*, or Commander of the Faithful, and exhibited piety and religious knowledge while assuming the responsibilities of appointing judges, supervising religious endowments, conducting jihad, leading Friday prayers, collecting taxes, and administering justice. Unlike the imams of twelver Shi'ite Islam, the Zaydi imam was not considered impeccable or infallible (*ma'sun*) and therefore his religious authority could be challenged. If after assuming the post of imam, the candidate was found to have lost one of these qualifications or had fallen short in the performance of his duties, he was expected to cede his position to a more qualified candidate. Similarly, Zaydis did not recognize a hereditary line of imams and were prepared to support any member of the upper social echelons of the Ahl al-Bayt who claimed the imamate and was elected by a council of *sayyids*.

The Zaydi imam was surrounded by the *ulema*, a council of advisers, who both interpreted tribal law and administered codes of public morality. The imam derived his legitimacy from the Zaydi ulema who in turn acted as mediators, administrators, and the country's principal bureaucracy. When revolts against Ottoman rule broke out during the 1880s, the rebellion was coordinated through this ad hoc governing body that acted both as intermediaries with the Ottoman sultan and as battlefield generals recruiting tribal armies.

When was Yemen first ruled by imams?

In the late 16th century, the Qasimi family gained control of the Zaydi imamate and staged a successful revolt against the Ottoman Empire. Prior to the departure of the first Ottoman state in Yemen, the Zaydi imams were usually confined territorially to the northern strongholds surrounding the city of Sa'dah. The secret of their longevity through numerous foreign dynasties since the 11th century CE was in the legitimacy retained in their religious authority based on traditional Islamic law and on their lineage as members of Ahl al-Bayt, or the Prophet Muhammad's household. The Qasimi imamate departed from this largely cloistered religious life following the departure of the Ottomans in 1635. Over the subsequent decades, Qasimi imams expanded the territory under their jurisdiction to include Dhofar in modern-day Oman, Asir and Najran in the north, and the Shafi'i territories of Lower Yemen, which brought additional tax revenue from agricultural produce and the sale of coffee in particular. These additional administrative responsibilities forced the evolution of the imam from a religious leader to a regional monarch who assumed the responsibility of a *muhtasib*, or the defender of his community from external aggression. For the first time, local Yemeni rulers needed to raise a standing army and formalize a bureaucracy that more closely resembled the modern Yemeni state. Loosely following the Ottoman administrative model, the Qasimi imams appointed local governors who assumed the responsibilities of collecting import duties and taxes and establishing a judicial system.

This institutionalization of the imamate during the Qasimi Dynasty through formalizing the customs, practices, and informal tribal governing organizations created, for the first time, a sense of a Yemeni state rather than a disparate group of tribes loosely controlled by a foreign power. An organized state required not only a standing army, which the Qasimi imams recruited primarily from Yemen's population of African slaves, but also a newly conceived model of dynastic succession that ensured the stability and rule of the Qasimi decedents. In violation of Zaydi tradition, Qasimi imams began appointing their sons in a dynastic succession that solidified their family's hold over leadership in the short term while stirring public ire in the long term for a Zaydi imamate that no longer represented the religious ideals espoused by earlier generations. The Qasimi line of imams lasted from 1716 to 1836, with each imam appointing his son as the governor of Sana'a and the commander of the armed forces and bestowing on him the title of Sayf al-Islam, or the Sword of Islam.

Beyond control over succession and military affairs, the Qasimi imams also founded their own mint, which was administered by Jewish artisans, to produce silver and copper coins both to propagate their titles and to exercise a degree of control over local commerce. In fact, the flourishing of the coffee trade under the Qasimi Dynasty provided the leadership with an income significant enough to allow the centralization of their state, earning them the nickname the "Coffee Imamate."

Was Yemen part of the Ottoman Empire?

The Ottomans first arrived in Yemen in the 16th century when Sultan Selim I conquered the western coast of Arabia, displacing the Egyptian Mamluk Empire, and declared himself the protector of Mecca and Medina, the two holiest sites in Islam. Selim I was confronted by the Portuguese, who had constructed their naval empire around strategically placed ports along the major oceanic routes, including the Arabian coast. During the 1540s, there was public fear that the Portuguese would force their way into the Red Sea port of Jeddah and capture Islam's holiest cities. As the sites' protector, the Ottoman sultan was under pressure to expand his dominion into Yemen in order to block a Portuguese invasion. The first Ottoman conquest of Yemen in 1569 was met with two decades of rebellion led by Imam al-Muttahar ibn Sharif al-Din, which forced the sultan to acquiesce to a peace arrangement that limited the extent of the Ottoman presence in the northern highlands until 1635. Local Yemeni rulers gradually won back greater autonomy from the Ottoman governor and eventually forced the Empire to retreat to the coastal regions, centered around the city of Zabid in the Tihama, where they maintained a continued presence until the arrival of the British in 1839.

International coffee trade attracted the interests of Dutch companies during the 17th century, followed in subsequent decades by British and American merchants seeking both agricultural wealth and access to strategic Red Sea harbors. For the British in particular, South Arabia constituted a vital cornerstone to securing their naval passage to India. British commercial interests and territorial expansion stood in direct contrast to Ottoman sovereignty in Arabia. The British seizure of Aden in 1839, in particular, convinced the Ottomans of a need to return to the northern highlands and consolidate their administration of the region as a check to British territorial and naval expansion. Similar to the 16th-century occupation of Yemen, Ottoman policy during the mid-19th century was a manifestation of their public responsibility as protectors of Islam's two holiest cities from Christian imperialists in Arabia. The British had in fact begun a process of encircling the Arabian Peninsula with naval bases, beginning with Oman in 1820 and ending with Kuwait in 1899. Aden was an important component of Britain's hegemony over the region's most important waterways: the Persian Gulf, the Gulf of Oman, and Bab al-Mandeb.

From 1849 through 1872, the Ottoman governor in Zabid extended his authority over the highlands through a series of costly military expeditions. The opening of the Suez Canal in 1869 served to stress the urgency and importance of Ottoman direct administration over North Yemen as a security gateway to one of the world's most important waterways. The implementation of *tanzimat* reforms across the Empire, or a liberalization of the state and courts based on a Western model, were rejected by Zaydi imams who perceived them as violations of Islamic shariah. Costly pacification of local tribal rebellions after 1872 was made more difficult by corrupt and incompetent administration and tax collection under officials appointed by Sultan Abdulhamid II (1876–1908). Rather than a security asset and source of tax revenue, Yemen became a military and financial burden for the Ottomans.

The Zaydi imamic rebellion was financed, not by local sources, but by an imperial rivalry that surrounded South Arabia. The Italians in Eritrea, the French in Djibouti, and the British in Aden were collectively accused of supporting anti-Ottoman forces and creating relative instability that would benefit their economic investments in Yemen's northern highlands. At the same time, Red Sea piracy precipitated numerous confrontations between the European empires and the Ottomans over responsibility for confronting the growing problem of naval brigands. The confrontations reached a crescendo in 1898 when the Italians threatened to seize Hodeidah in order to root out the marauding pirates there. The final rebellion against Ottoman rule was led by Imam Yahya Hamid al-Din (1904–1948) who led his countrymen through seven years of civil war culminating in de facto independence in 1911.

When did the British first arrive in Yemen?

The "sun never sets on the British Empire" went the mantra during the 19th century. To get from one end of the empire to the other, however, the British navy needed ports in the vicinity of Yemen, the gateway to the Red Sea. Before settling on Aden, British officials tested the waters around Mocha and the island of Prim in search of an ideal harbor and site for a naval base.

Although Aden was the largest and most famous, it was not the first British-administered port in Yemen. This title can be given to Mocha where the British expanded the natural harbor before being driven out by the Ottomans. The port city of Mocha was a major marketplace for coffee between the 15th and 18th centuries, thus bestowing its name to the contemporary coffee flavor. When the first British ships visited Aden in 1609, the crew was greeted with Ottoman hostility and found a commercial center that had been greatly diminished by the ongoing Ottoman-Portuguese conflict. The British East India Company chose instead to establish a trading post in Mocha in 1618 and were followed by the Dutch and French East India Companies in later decades. By 1800, even American merchants had arrived in Mocha and they became the main exporters of Yemeni coffee.

With the British Navy's gradual adaptation of steam-powered boats in the 19th century, convenient coaling stations became increasingly important for imperial communication, particularly along the route from Bombay to Suez. The geographic and strategic assets of Yemen's coastline factored into the strategic calculations of British naval officers and merchants at the turn of the 19th century. The British navy first tried utilizing the southern port of Mukalla along the Hadrami coast, established a coal depot on the Egyptian-held island of Kamaran (northwest of Hodeidah), and even tried to buy the island of Soqotra off the Horn of Africa. It was not until 1837 that British colonial authorities in India finally settled on Aden, which was situated midway between India and Egypt. This decision was partially driven by British efforts to subvert American merchants who had since developed a monopoly on Yemeni trade through the port of Mocha.

In 1837, British Captain S. B. Haines orchestrated an international incident that involved locals seizing the cargo and passengers of a British merchant ship that had crashed into the rocky shores surrounding Aden. In retribution, Haines captured Aden two years later and presented the port as a gift to Queen Victoria, in what was her first official colonial possession. The British occupied Aden in January 1839, with the intention of establishing a refueling port between Suez and India and preventing Egypt's Muhammad Ali from conquering all of South Arabia. What began as a coaling station for the British navy eventually served as a strategic link in Britain's imperial communications and ultimately as a reflection of the rise and fall of Britain's global empire.

The events of 1837–1839 and the British seizure of Aden were fundamental in the history that both transformed the South Arabian economy and brought the region under the aegis of modern European colonialism. Under the British, major construction expanded port facilities and related service industries, making Aden, by the 1950s, one of the world's largest and busiest natural harbors. The port became a major coal refueling station for Indian Ocean traffic sailing to and from the Suez Canal and later evolved into a hub for the petroleum market as the British Petroleum company constructed a large refinery and headquarters in Aden.

When did Yemen gain its independence?

When Imam Yahya of the Hamid al-Din family declared North Yemen independent from the Ottoman Empire on October 30, 1918, the Mutawakkilite Kingdom of Yemen became the first independent Arab state in the Middle East. Imam Yahya's rebellion from 1904 to 1911 was only the last in five decades of Zaydi rebellion against the Ottoman Empire. The imam had the unanimous support of the Zaydi ulema, or religious council, who saw the rebellions as defending Zaydi religious rights against a modernizing Ottoman Empire. As was the case during Roman times, the mountains of northern Yemen heavily favored the defending tribesmen and made an Ottoman reconquest of the highlands nearly impossible. In fact, during the tribal siege of Sana'a in 1905, the Ottomans suffered an estimated 10,000 casualties. It was not for naught that the northern highlands of Yemen, a terrain that has and continues to favor the native population, were known as the "graveyard of the Turks," just as Afghanistan earned the title the "graveyard of empires."

In 1911, both sides signed a final truce at Da'an, named for a small village in the Sana'a governorate. In addition to growing frustration with the failed campaign in Yemen, in 1911 the Italians had invaded Libya, an Ottoman province in North Africa, thus further distracting Ottoman attention away from the Red Sea. Imam Yahya preserved the region's sovereign rights while pledging loyalty to the Ottoman Empire, a pledge that would end in 1918 after the end of the First World War. Yahya also had designs on the northern region of 'Asir, which at the time was under the rule of the Idrisi Emirate. By establishing a temporary hiatus from a costly conflict with the Ottoman Empire, Yahya obtained the freedom to expand his territory and power locally. This 'Asir region would later factor into Saudi-Yemeni relations given its position along the border between the two countries.

South Yemen, on the other hand, did not gain independence until 1967 when the British withdrew from Aden. Colonial officials had envisioned a Federation of South Arabia with representatives from each tribal area. The National Liberation Front, the principal opponents of British colonialism, seized power and formed the first and only Arab communist state.

What kind of government first ruled Yemen after independence?

Imam Yahya used his nationalist popularity and religious credentials to centralize the northern Yemeni state and consolidate authority around the imam. His popular image as an anti-imperial champion would take Yahya only so far in countering the many tribal families who coveted the position of imam. To assure his rule as imam, Yahya held a son from each sheikh's family in Sana'a as a hostage and as collateral for ensuring the loyalty of the represented tribe. Hostage-taking was part of a concerted effort to divide and rule the surrounding tribes by maintaining an atmosphere of mistrust and power intrigue. With the willing and coerced allegiance of the northern tribes, Yahya sought to protect his country from modernist reforms, democratization, and economic modernizations that he perceived as threats to Islamic society that would eventually draw Yemen once again under the dominance of an imperial power. Without foreign investment, however, Yemen's infrastructure, education, and health services were severely lacking, even while the Imam's taxes were onerous. In an effort to prolong the rule of his Hamid al-Din family, Yahya named his son Ahmad as Crown Prince, challenging rules of succession by introducing primogeniture to a process normally controlled by a council of Zaydi notables.

North Yemen under the rule of the Hamid al-Din family, which included Imams Yahya (1904–1948), Ahmad (1948–1962), and Muhammad al-Badr (1962–1970), did not resemble the powerful imams of the Qasimi Dynasty. Rather than centralized armies and powerful religious courts, the Hamid al-Dins administered their constituents with a very meticulous and personal approach, preferring not to leave even minor and local matters to the jurisdiction of others. The micromanagement of the Hamid al-Dins allowed them to retain strict control over tribal leadership and territory, either by retaining hostages in Sana'a or delivering strategic subsidies to tribal sheikhs in exchange for their loyalty. The loss of 'Asir, Najran, and Jizan, three border regions, to Ibn Saud of Saudi Arabia in 1933, called the power of the Hamid al-Din leadership into question and officially marked the start of an opposition movement to the imamate. The decision made by Yahya and Ahmad to respond to the 1933 military defeat at the hands of Saudi Arabia with the creation of a national army was ultimately the family's downfall.

Historians have often criticized Yahya for cutting Yemen off from modernity, citing his arcane methods of rule as evidence. The imam is often quoted as saying that "if I have to choose between being rich but dependent and poor but independent, I will choose the latter." Rather than two decades of isolation under Imam Yahya, Yemen played a prominent role in regional foreign affairs during the 1920s and 1930s. As a testament to Yemen's geographical importance to Red Sea trade and security, it signed treaties with the Soviets (1928), the Italians (1926—Treaty of Sana'a), the British (1934), and Ibn Saud (1934—Treaty of Taif). Yet it was Yahya's defeat at the hands of Saudi Arabia in 1933 that first caused him alarm as to the disturbing unreadiness of Yemen's small tribal militias to stand up against rapidly modernizing global militaries. Recognizing Yemen's lack of military leadership and civil servants convinced Imam Yahya to sponsor a small contingent of carefully selected pupils to study abroad in Egypt, Iraq, Europe, and the United States. Known as the Famous Forty, this initial group of students sent abroad would form the core of the modern Yemeni republic that emerged in 1962 after overthrowing the imamate. These very same teenage students sent for study abroad returned as officers in the army of the Mutawakkilite Kingdom of Yemen and formed the core of the military coup that would overthrow Imam Muhammad al-Badr in 1962, marking the beginning of a civil war that would end the Hamid al-Din imamate. Yahya's fears of foreign domination and warnings over the dangers of modernization were posthumously realized less than 15 years after his death.

In 1948, Yahya was killed in a coup orchestrated by the rival al-Wazir family. This revolution lasted less than four months as the populace was shocked by the murder of a religious leader, an act that had previously been taboo. Yahya's son Ahmad had been in the southern city of Ta'iz at the time and managed to gather loyal tribes and reestablish the imamate, albeit with a capital moved to Ta'iz. Stories of Ahmad's post-coup heroism and his ability to survive multiple assassination attempts during the 1950s gave him an aura of invincibility and respect, strengthened by his appearance—his large bulging eyes instilled a sense of fear in all those who gazed on him. Rather than follow the precedents of his father, Ahmad was open to reforming the Yemeni Kingdom by allying with the Soviets and Chinese and allowing them to build major roads, a port in Hodeidah, and an airport in Sana'a. Along with Chinese construction teams and Yugoslav engineers, Ahmad received advanced weaponry from the Soviet Union including T34 tanks, aircraft, field artillery, and anti-aircraft guns. Lacking the expertise to use and maintain this arsenal and fearing it would be used against him in a coup, Ahmad dismantled the munitions and dispersed their parts to warehouses and caves around the country. During the 1960s, the Egyptian military would discover, much to their chagrin, that the only way to transport Ahmad's hidden artillery shells was on the backs of donkeys along steep mountainous paths.

Is there a social hierarchy in Yemeni society? How has that evolved over the centuries?

Race, equality, and social mobility are contentious topics in contemporary American society where many assume that these issues are unique to the United States. In fact, the strata and hierarchy within Yemeni society are far more rigid than those in the United States. At the top of the social ladder is a group known as the *sadah* or *sayyid* in singular, who can trace their ancestral lineage back to the Prophet Muhammad. According to historical tradition, these families in Yemen migrated from the Sunni-dominated Hijaz to southwestern Arabia, likely at the behest of feuding tribes who sought religious mediation. Within these sayyid families, there are also subgroups known as *bayt*, or house, that identify with a prominent ancestor. For centuries, sadah constituted the country's aristocracy, filling the ranks of imams, the ulama, and the qadis, or religious judges. Sadah expected and were given social and financial support to dedicate their lives to education, both religious and scientific, in their pursuit of knowledge and literature. Marriage to a non-sayyid, especially by women who were not in a position to continue patrilineal genealogical lines, was forbidden by the imam as it would otherwise violate the sanctity of ahl al-Bayt, or the people of the house.

The social hierarchy crumbled following the establishment of a republic in 1962 as sadah fell from their positions of leadership and were subject to the jurisdiction of the republic and derision at the hands of the non-sayyid population. Bayt Hamid al-Din, the ruling royal house of Muhammad al-Badr, the last imam of Yemen, was forced into exile while the estates of other major sayyid families were confiscated. The republican government legislation withdrew recognition of a distinct sayyid social class and did not reserve special places for sadah in politics. Even the imam's restriction on marriage was lifted de jure and de facto, bringing about a growing number of mixed marriages between sayyid and non-sayyid families. Post-revolutionary sadah families still prioritize education but have since ventured into previously taboo fields of commerce, agriculture, and craftsmanship. A century of imams along with their sadah class have been demonized by contemporary media, perpetuating the sense that they are a distinct class even as the public acts to eliminate notions of social classes. There remains an inherent mistrust within the republic's government of the sayyid class, out of fear that they retain designs on restoring the imamate and the social dominance of the sadah. These fears, often vocalized by the Saleh administration during the early battles against the Houthi revolt in the city of Sa'dah since 2004, have since come to fruition as the Houthis, a sayyid family, seized the capital city of Sana'a in part to restore the traditional positions of the northern tribal families, including those of the sayyid class.

At the other end of the social spectrum were two classes of servants known as *khaddam* and *akhdam*, both deriving from the Arabic root which means "to serve." The khaddam are Yemeni in origin but were born into a subordinate social position and relegated to the service industry such as house cooks, *mulahhin* (singers), drivers, and construction workers. The *muzayyin* are a subgroup of khaddam consisting of butchers, barbers, bath attendants, messengers, and growers of vegetables. According to historical lore, the khaddam were members of tribes defeated in battle and stripped of social status and the right to own personal property. After the 1962 revolution, many khaddam families migrated to Saudi Arabia and the Gulf, entering into myriad trades in the oil fields and the related economic boom, leaving their lower social status behind in Yemen. At the absolute bottom of the social ladder were the *ahkdam*, meaning "black slaves," constituting an estimated 3% of the population, who were relegated to socially marginalized professions such as street sweepers, cesspool cleaners, and other jobs seen as beneath the dignity of native Yemenis. Most of the akhdam have darker skin, tracing their lineage back to either the invading troops of Abyssinia or centuries of the Omani slave trade. There are between

200,000 and 1 million ahkdam living in Yemen today, with many having migrated to urban areas in search of meager employment or roaming the streets begging. A growing number of akhdam have been forced to live in shanty houses in the slum outskirts of major cities like Sana'a and Ta'iz.

Government officials and local civil society organizations have been reluctant to improve the condition of the akhdam, preferring to maintain the status quo in a society jaded by social and racial prejudice. During the 1990s, several European governments provided funding for Yemeni nongovernmental organizations (NGOs) to provide housing and secure garbage removal jobs for the akhdam population. Their employers mandated an orange jumpsuit as part of the uniform, a conspicuous colored outfit which unintentionally became a further symbol of their inferior social condition. As late as 2010, the Yemeni government continued to perpetuate the false generalization that their country has no ethnic groups and is entirely homogenous, when in fact Yemen has longstanding and institutionalized racism based on loose historical backgrounds and skin color.

What does it mean to be a Yemeni?

Yemenis and South Arabians more generally consider themselves decedents of a shared biblical ancestor of Qahtan. As a unifying factor, this common identity also serves to exclude those Yemenis who do not fit the same historical narrative. Khaddam and Akkhdam, the bottom of the social hierarchy are victims of this ancestral supremacy. The same is true for immigrants from India, Somalia, and Ethiopia who are not accepted into mainstream society even after several generations of residence in Yemen. Residents of the Yemeni island of Soqotra are often considered foreigners and adhering to a different historical heritage that traces its origins to a Greek settlement established by Alexander the Great in the 4th century BCE. Even the Jews of Yemen, whose presence in the country is recognized as one of the most ancient and historically authentic, are still afforded a diminished secondary status, both a manifestation of religious differences and a distinct ancestral tradition.

When the Yemeni republic was created in 1962, the state sought to eliminate the fissures within this socially fragmented society through the inauguration of Yemeni citizenship. A civil war between the old and new generations of Yemeni identity, however, pitted the northern Zaydi tribesmen against the urban and secularist republican revolutionaries. After the war was over in 1970, the shared Qahtani ancestry was turned against the northern tribesmen in an effort to exclude them from the new government. Specifically targeting the sadah social class, the revolutionaries accused the Zaydis of belonging to the lineage of 'Adnan, the ancestor of Northern Arabia. Where Qahtan was a direct descendant of Noah's children, 'Adnan is considered a direct descendant of biblical Abraham's son Ishmael. Northern Zaydis were thus ostracized as foreigners who arrived in the 9th century to colonize South Arabia, thus portraying them as agents of Saudi domination. The 'Adnani-Qahtani ancestral rivalry has further soured the unity of a fractious state still struggling to find its identity.

In South Yemen, residents are united behind a shared experience and modern sense of nationalism that at times transcends even the adherence to tribal affiliation. There were few moments in the history of independent South Yemen that southerners can uphold with pride. The 1970s and the bloody civil war in 1986 were defined by ruthless brutality, foreign intervention in southern politics, and a siege mentality owing to the country's regional isolation. Between bouts of carnage, a remnant of the anti-colonial struggle fought by the National Liberation Front (NLF), there were indeed golden eras for the south that reinforced the feeling of southern exceptionalism, a separate identity from that espoused by North Yemenis. Southern secular and non-tribal identity, superior educational opportunities, healthcare, and economic development are often touted as the major differences between South and North Yemen during the post-colonial era.

Yemeni nationalism as a concept is wholly a 20th-century construct, one that needed to be occasionally modified based on South Arabian geography and history. North and South Yemen constructed their own post-independence narratives that needed to be hastily combined when the two united in 1990. North and South are not, however, a single homogenous identity. The North is divided between the traditional Zaydis highlands, the Shafi'i lowlands, and the Tihama coastal area. The South is often portrayed as a country with six self-governing regions: Abyan, Lahej, Aden, Shabwa, Hadramawt, and al-Mahra. What emerges from these varied and often contentious sets of identities is only a loose sense of what it means to be a Yemeni—other than the words on the cover of one's passport.

4

AN ERA OF MODERNIZATION— THE FORMATION OF THE YEMENI REPUBLIC

In faith and love, I am part of mankind,
And I shall march first among the Arabs.
And my heartbeat shall remain that of a Yemenite.
No foreigner shall ever hold dominion over Yemen.
—Abdullah Nu'man (1917–1982), "Original Yemeni
National Anthem"

When was the modern Yemeni state founded?

Arab nationalism emerged during the 1950s as a dominant political movement across the Middle East and North Africa. Championed by Egyptian president Gamal Abdel Nasser, nationalist movements gradually supplanted religious and tribal identities and in the process overthrew a generation of post-colonial monarchs and theocrats. North Yemen was no exception to the Arab nationalist fervor that came to dominate the region's politics through the 1960s.

Muhammad al-Badr, the last imam of the Mutawakkilite Kingdom of Yemen, assumed the throne after the death of his father Ahmad, on September 19, 1962. One week later, on September 26, al-Badr's royal palace was attacked and the Yemen Arab Republic was declared in place of an imamate by a coalition of military commanders modeling themselves on Egypt's Free Officers Movement. The anniversary of the September 26 revolution, which remains one of the most celebrated holidays in Yemen, created for the first time a sense of Yemeni national identity that transcended the regional and tribal allegiances that had long dominated the country.

The events of 1962 were the culmination of 15 years of revolutionary machinations by a growing minority of northern Yemen's population that was disillusioned with the rule of the Hamid al-Din family. At the center of this revolutionary movement was a group of Yemeni students known as the Famous Forty who were sent abroad for education at government expense. Envisioned as the country's next generation of modern civil servants and army administration, these forty students were instead exposed to Arab nationalist ideas in Egypt and Iraq and advanced Western societies in Europe and the United States, which they contrasted with the relative backwardness of the Mutawakkilite Kingdom of Yemen. They were joined by hundreds of other Yemenis studying abroad during the 1950s, who returned home to Yemen fomenting civil unrest across the country that manifested itself in the assassination of Imam Yahya in 1948 and numerous attacks on Imam Ahmad during the 1950s.

September 1962 was the final stage of this 15-year revolution that managed to overthrow not only the imam but also the entire institution of the imamate. What started as a local regime change in a remote country far removed from the Cold War was transformed into a global arena of conflict that overran North and South Yemen for the six years during a civil war that transformed southern Arabia.

Who participated in the first Yemeni civil war?

The coup in September 1962 succeeded where earlier attempts had failed precisely because the central organizers were able to secure international recognition for the fledgling Yemeni republic. A small delegation of Yemeni revolutionaries arrived in Cairo at the behest of the Abdullah Sallal, the first president of the Yemen Arab Republic and persuaded President Gamal Abdel Nasser of Egypt to commit Egyptian troops in support of what Nasser perceived as the newest member of the Arab nationalist coalition. What began with a battalion soon ballooned into an army of 70,000 soldiers, mired in what Nasser termed "my Vietnam."

The Egyptian army was faced with a fierce guerilla campaign orchestrated by a coalition of tribal armies aligned with the deposed Imam Muhammad al-Badr, who had escaped the shelling of his palace in Sana'a. Al-Badr secured the financial support of the Saudi monarchy whose members were alarmed by the belligerency of the new Yemeni republic and the prospect of an Egyptian presence in South Arabia. Neither Abdullah Sallal nor Gamal Abdel Nasser made any effort to disguise the fact that they coveted Saudi oil wealth and territory, leaving Saudi Arabia with little choice but to support the northern tribal coalition standing between the Saudi Kingdom and a menacing Egyptian army.

What emerged during the 1960s was a local Yemeni civil war overrun by the regional powers of Egypt and Saudi Arabia and by the political intricacies of the international Cold War. Mired in its own Vietnam War, the United States committed few resources to this remote conflict and even emerged on the same side of the civil war as the Soviet Union when President Kennedy belatedly recognized the Yemen Arab Republic (YAR) in December 1962. The Soviet Union (USSR), on the other hand, used the civil war to cultivate patrons in South Arabia with the ultimate goal of establishing a permanent Soviet naval presence in the vital Bab al-Mandeb straits.

International diplomatic efforts were slow to materialize, largely because the United Nations (UN) peacekeeping portfolio was faced with a funding crisis following the cost overruns of the missions to Congo and Sinai. Reluctance to fund future peacekeeping missions was a manifestation of European unease with the gradual inclusion of post-colonial nations in the UN General Assembly and the growing strength of the Asia-Africa voting bloc and the overall Non-Aligned Movement. U Thant, the UN secretary general during the Yemen Civil War, was limited in his freedom of action by these contentious sentiments among world leaders. The UN Yemen Observer Mission (UNYOM) from 1963 to 1964 was the first example of "tin-cup" peacekeeping, run with a minimalist budget and funded by the belligerent parties themselves. Although UNYOM failed to bring the war to an end, it successfully oversaw a temporary demilitarized zone between Yemen and Saudi Arabia, the model of which has been discussed as a potential component of a comprehensive solution to the 2015 crisis.

What impact did the civil war have on the rest of the Middle East?

When Nasser dubbed Yemen "his Vietnam," he may not have realized how prophetic that statement would turn out to be. Egypt's army was locked in an unwinnable war against a tribal guerilla force entrenched in the northern mountainous regions of Yemen, the same topography that defeated the Roman and Ottoman Empires. The drain on Egypt's resources was coupled with a concurrent decline in Nasser's prestige. The once ardent Arab Nationalist leader had unsuccessfully refocused his attention on another Arab country rather than on his broader conflict with European colonialists. Few realized at the time that Nasser's presence in Yemen was indeed part of his struggle against the British, a struggle that would usher in the ultimate decline of both the British Empire and Arab nationalism.

Nasser used his advantageous position in North Yemen to support the Front for the Liberation of South Yemen (FLOSY), an anti-colonial military and political organization opposing the British presence in Aden. Although FLOSY did not emerge as the victorious champions that Nasser envisioned, it was Egypt's very presence on the peninsula that inspired the southern revolt and pressured British colonial authorities. The rebels of the southern Radfan region, nicknamed the Red Wolves of Yemen, sparked an armed revolution against British Aden on October 14, 1963, marking the date as both the beginning of the Aden Emergency and the date marking southern independence, annually celebrated in South Yemen ever since. Four years after the first shots were fired in Radfan, the last British soldier left Aden, which had been the last outpost of British imperial and military power in the Middle East. Just as the seizure of Aden in 1839 marked the beginning of British preeminence in the Middle East, the British departure from Aden in 1967 marked the end of British hegemony in the region, ushering in a power vacuum that would be filled by competing international powers and ideologies.

The economic strain of the Yemen Civil War and the gradual increase in anti-Egyptian sentiments in the international community began exerting pressure on Nasser to either achieve victory in Yemen or retreat to Egypt in preparation for a Sinai border campaign with Israel. Egyptian withdrawal from the conflict was delayed many times, including a last-minute decision by Nasser in 1966 to retain troops in South Arabia until the British left. Ultimately, Nasser's hand would be forced by events along the Sinai border, and the last Egyptian soldier would withdraw soon after the last British soldier left Aden at the end of 1967.

Perhaps the most significant impact of the Yemen Civil War on the rest of the Middle East was related to the June 1967 war between Israel and Egypt. Unbeknownst to Nasser, a group of Israeli pilots, navigators, and intelligence agents operated in Yemen and became one of the most significant suppliers to Imam al-Badr's guerilla campaign against Egypt. This involvement gave Israel a ringside seat to the performance of the Egyptian army, Israel's principal border threat at the time.

Egypt's military, trained primarily for desert warfare in Sinai, was faced with an unfamiliar and mountainous terrain that proved an insurmountable obstacle to a mechanized army. Nasser's growing reliance on air power proved only minimally effective, as a vast system of caves underlying the mountainous terrain acted as a natural bunker for Yemeni tribal militias and their artillery. The Egyptian air force began experimenting with improvised tear gas grenades in 1963 and then expanded into an extensive poison gas campaign against Yemen's cave network in January 1967. Egypt's chemical warfare received scant condemnation as the international community was far more interested in the herbicidal campaign in Vietnam. Israel, however, was alarmed by Egypt's unchecked use of chemical weapons, depicting this menacing method of warfare as an existential threat to their own citizens. The fear of chemical weapons added to the growing list of reasons for Israel's preemptive strike on Egypt's airfields in June 1967.

Egyptian generals later blamed the Yemen Civil War as one of the main reasons the country's army was unprepared for a border war with Israel. While the absence of troops, planes, and resources may or may not have changed the eventual outcome in June 1967, the actual outbreak of the war may be traced to Egypt's use of chemical weapons in Yemen and the global complacency with Egyptian militant expansionism. The 1960s civil war in Yemen served to upend the Middle East, contributing to the downfalls of the regional British Empire and Egypt-led Arab Nationalism, and sparking the June 1967 war that transformed the Israel-Palestine conflict for the subsequent decades.

What happened during the siege of Sana'a in 1968 to make it so important?

By the end of 1967, the last Egyptian troops had been withdrawn from Yemen, leaving the Yemeni republic without the support of

70,000 Egyptian soldiers nor the benefit of an advanced air force. The northern tribal armies, allied with Imam al-Badr, marched on Sana'a in November 1967, placing the capital city under siege. As 65,000 tribesmen approached, YAR president Abdullah Sallal was overthrown in a bloodless coup, a fact that was made known to him only after his plane touched down in the Baghdad airport. Sallal was replaced by Abdul Rahman Iryani as president and Hassan al-Amri as general. Iryani, a religious judge or *qadi*, was the only civilian YAR president, as those who preceded and succeeded him all held senior military ranks. Al-Amri was the most senior member of the leadership who stayed behind during the siege and earned mythical status as a Yemeni hero of the revolution. In fact, every defender of Sana'a was immortalized in the pantheon of Yemeni revolutionary history, including Ali Abdullah Saleh, whose biography claims that he was serving in the republican army during the siege.

Although fighting continued for another two years, the republican victory after a 70-day siege constituted a victory in the civil war. As a result of decisions made by al-Amri during and after republican forces declared victory in February 1968, North Yemeni politics shifted decisively from the socialist policies advocated by Nasser and toward a far more conservative leadership. Al-Amri, who viewed Nasser's military presence in Yemen with disdain, mistrusted Egypt's collaborators and sought to rid the YAR of socialist elements, including those who aided his defense of Sana'a only months earlier. Further encouraging this move toward the right was Saudi Arabia's agreement to withdraw funding from Imam al-Badr and the royalists only if the YAR embraced an "Islamic" identity rather than a socialist and Arab nationalist ethos. Zaydi northern tribesmen were more willing to accept a conservative and religious republic than one with a Sunni and socialist leadership. The late historian Fred Halliday referred to this emerging republican coalition in 1970 as "tribalist republicans," a reflection of the political power retained by the northern tribal leaders in the new government.

In 1970, Imam Muhammad al-Badr finally conceded in a momentous speech. He agreed to abdicate and live in exile in order to save Yemen. The Hamid al-Din ruling family left en masse and its members resettled variously in Kent, England; Saudi Arabia; and other Middle Eastern countries. With the downfall of the Zaydi Imamate, the longest serving Hashemite dynasty came to an end, marking a major transition for the country's elite class of sadah. The same genealogies connecting sadah with the Prophet Muhammad that had once been a source of legitimacy for the ruling elite had become a source of ridicule and derision in the modern republic.

Who succeeded the first YAR president and what kind of government emerged during the 1970s?

After Sallal was overthrown in 1967, Abdul Rahman al-Iryani became president and oversaw an end to the civil war and the formation of a coalition government consisting of northern tribesmen and members of the republican leadership. In the aftermath of this costly civil war, however, the YAR lagged far behind the rest of the developing world in basic infrastructure and modern facilities for health and services. During the 1970s, the YAR was the recipient of assistance from Saudi Arabia, Kuwait, the US Agency for International Development (AID), and several European countries. The Saudis established a precedent that would continue for the next four decades, of both funding the central government and providing regular stipends to tribal sheikhs in exchange for their loyalty.

This Saudi policy was put to the test in 1973 when the YAR was mired in a crippling budget shortfall. Prime Minister Abdullah al-Hajri negotiated state-to-state cash payments from Saudi Arabia to cover budgetary deficits, which amounted to over $25 million in direct aid. Saudi money and increased remittances from Yemeni workers abroad solved the short-term budgetary crisis. At the same time, foreign aid, particularly from West Germany, the United States, the World Bank, USAID, and other Gulf States, was used to finance capital development in transportation and communications—for example, a new Sana'a airport, highways, government buildings, and the Tihama Development Authority. The government's Central Planning Organization embarked on a program to recruit foreign-trained Yemenis from abroad to return and oversee national development.

A bloodless coup on June 13, 1974, replaced Iryani with the Command Council headed by Ibrahim Muhammad al-Hamdi, who was accompanied by Sinan Abu Luhum and other tribal leaders who had the blessing of Saudi Arabia in orchestrating this change in government. Hamdi was in his mid-30s at the time of the coup, the son of a respected Zaydi qadi, and had served as commander of an elite military unit and deputy prime minister. In 1975, Hamdi dismissed his former boss, Prime Minister Mohsin al-Aini, and dissolved the Command Council in an effort to curtail the national power of tribal leaders. Hamdi also targeted Sinan abu Luhum and the Luhumi clan of the Bakil Federation, by forcing four Luhumi family members to resign from the army.

When tribal elements gathered in the Arhab region to oppose Hamdi's regime, he ordered an armed assault and forced the responsible local sheikhs to pledge allegiance to his regime in Sana'a. This strong-arm tactic became known as the "Arhab" model, as it marked a departure from state acquiescence to tribal authority and the beginnings of a centralized state and army. The expansion and consolidation of the YAR armed forces was funded, in part, by military assistance from the United States. Hamdi was North Yemen's first populist, modeling himself after the famous Egyptian populist leader Gamal Abdel Nasser. Rather than rely on a Nasser-like cult of personality, Hamdi created a sense of modern Yemeni national identity that was not divided into sayyid versus non-sayyid and tribal versus non-tribal factions. He upheld a ban on political parties, while calling for national elections that never came to fruition. Young Yemenis at the time credited him with saving the YAR from sectarianism like the "Lebanese Model" of perpetual religious conflict. Holidays like the National Tree Day, for example, came to personify Hamdi and his regime and how it inspired a new generation of Yemenis to invest in a better and more prosperous Yemen.

Hamdi was equally ambitious in his foreign policy. He sought to unify the two Yemens and exact greater concessions and autonomy from Saudi Arabia. His first official foreign visit to Saudi Arabia in July 1974, less than three weeks after coming to power, would be followed by three more visits in 1975 as Hamdi persuaded the Saudis to end tribal subsidies and instead fund US weapons purchases for the YAR army. This led to the creation of the Saudi-Yemeni Joint Coordinating Council with a $273 million initial pledge of budget subsidies and development loans, to be reevaluated annually based on YAR development needs. Saudi Arabia financed an arms purchase from the United States, contingent upon Hamdi expelling Soviet military advisers from the country, a stipulation no doubt added by United States officials. At the same time, Hamdi sought closer ties with the People's Democratic Republic of Yemen (PDRY) to avoid a leftist armed rebellion against YAR. He held joint meetings on unification with PDRY leader Salim Rubaya Ali in 1977 and began preparations to travel to Aden to celebrate the October 14 Revolution Anniversary.

Hamdi introduced the concept of "Red Sea security" as leverage to secure grants and concessions from Saudi Arabia, whose leaders had concerns with Ethiopia's decision to join the socialist camp. The Saudis consistently delayed in paying for weapons shipments because of their concern that Hamdi might threaten the Saudi Kingdom by introducing radical regime change in Yemen; this gave rise to a well-known joke at the time that the Saudis had agreed to finance the purchase of tanks only when a tank was invented that could drive and shoot south but not north! Hamdi's ability to balance political forces both domestically and abroad eventually also became the hallmark of his successor, Ali Abdullah Saleh.

How did Ibrahim al-Hamdi transform North Yemen?

Hamdi's greatest and most long-lasting impact on Yemen was his modernization of state institutions. Even before becoming president, Hamdi had consolidated the self-help construction projects of the local development associations (LDAs) into the Confederation of Yemeni Development Associations, a centralized state authority for the construction of schools, roads, and hospitals, funded by international aid and increased worker remittances. In particular, the Tihama Development Authority and the Wadi Zabid Project (1977) oversaw a large-scale upgrade of rural development through expanded irrigation and provision of modern agricultural equipment. Both of these Hamdi-led initiatives were considered high points of development models in Yemen.

Under Hamdi, the YAR legal system was modernized, marking a departure from courts formerly guided by the traditional *shariah* legal framework, with the introduction of a judiciary guided by secular state legislation. Hamdi's judicial reform was coupled with a modernization of the country's civil service, assisted by the UN Development Program (UNDP) and an International Monetary Fund–led reform of the YAR system of taxation to access new sources of tax revenue, reduce inefficiency, and protect against corruption. Dr. Abdul Karim al-Iryani, who earned his PhD in biochemical genetics from Yale University, was appointed minister of education in 1976. His ambition was to modernize the traditional education system and devote additional teaching hours to math and science. Although al-Iryani's proposals were opposed by both religious leaders in Yemen and religious conservatives in Saudi Arabia, Iryani's ambition and optimism for the development of education in Yemen cemented his place in the YAR and, later, as part of Saleh's regime.

Hamdi fell short in his effort to corral the northern tribes into the centralized state after centuries of relative independence. He had too much confidence in his national popularity and made only modest attempts to organize political support in the standoff between the state and the tribes. In 1977, the deposed Sinan abu Luhum organized a group of northern tribal leaders to oppose Hamdi, whom they labeled a "communist and atheist." The tribal opposition finally succeeded in dethroning Hamdi on October 11, 1977, after his body was discovered together with the corpses of his brother Abdullah and two unnamed French women (believed to be prostitutes) in a private house on the outskirts of Sana'a. Hamdi had managed to accumulate many enemies, including the tribal leaders who distrusted his intentions and the Saudis who were concerned that Hamdi was becoming a "little Nasser." During his short-lived presidency, Hamdi had ousted the tribal opposition and dismantled the Yemeni political system but had failed to construct an alternative. Hamdi had announced his plans to form a General People's Congress (GPC) in 1977, but this foundational political organization would have to wait to be realized until the presidency of Ali Abdullah Saleh. Across generations, Yemenis remember Hamdi as a true nationalist and as a faint glimmer of hope for a Yemeni state not dominated by tribal interests or the whims of foreign powers.

What kind of state emerged after the British withdrew from South Yemen in 1967?

During an occupation that lasted from 1839 until 1967, the British developed the port city of Aden economically, politically, and judicially.

Colonial influence spread beyond the city borders to the immediate hinterland through multiple treaties of protection and influence that had been signed by all the surrounding tribes by 1954, forming an East and a West Aden Protectorate. This area, surrounding the port of Aden, was to become the People's Democratic Republic of Yemen (PDRY) following the British withdrawal.

Like other British colonial structures, Aden was divided into two legal districts. The British-sanctioned qadis of Aden and Sheikh Othman were given authority over religious matters of marriage, divorce, and the Islamic calendar, while the British maintained legal jurisdiction over everything else. The often-tense relationship between religious qadis and British colonial authority was exemplified by protracted disputes emanating from the British campaign against child marriage, a widespread practice in Aden. The qadis were not united in their opposition to British legal authority and often preferred to manipulate British "colonial shariah" to their personal advantage rather than toward a collective goal.

British administration of the protectorates preserved native institutions in an effort to systematize administrative and judicial procedures while contributing to a gradual tribal modernization. British colonial rule relied heavily on agents of colonialism. British colonial control of the Western Aden Protectorate, in particular, was dependent on the allegiance of tribal rulers. Local sheikhs and tribal leaders were given stipends to maintain order and show deference to British colonial authority in Aden, a practice that undermined their local legitimacy and made them vulnerable to later state centralization under the PDRY. When the British left in 1967, these tribal leaders were seen by Yemeni nationalists as willing collaborators with the imperialist overlords. Some were executed while others were removed from power in a series of actions that weakened cohesion in southern Yemen. In an effort to foster nationalist sentiment in South Yemen, the use of tribal names was abolished, bearing arms—including the traditional *jambiya* ceremonial dagger—was banned, and clubs and organizations based on tribal affiliations were permanently closed. The old generation of tribal sheikhs was replaced by a new generation of National Liberation Front (NLF) party members who exercised local governance and authority.

Following the withdrawal of the last British troops on November 29, 1967, the leaders of the NLF who had led the successful anti-colonial campaign declared a People's Republic of Southern Yemen, the first and only Marxist state in the Arab world. The Soviet Union eventually committed to supporting the new state, which was renamed the People's Democratic Republic of Yemen and which was run by a strong centralized state, army, and police force. The USSR was particularly interested in the Aden port facilities because of their strategic naval location and proximity to the Arabian oil fields. One hundred thirty years of British colonial occupation had fostered a progressive society that boasted education and health facilities superior to those of their northern counterparts, especially within the urban confines of Aden. In contrast to the northern tribal communities, women in the PDRY had access to education, professional careers, and protective family laws. This unique and open society acted as a magnet for international terrorist organizations and revolutionary movements, such as the Popular Front for the Liberation of Palestine, the Irish Republican Army, the Red Brigade, Baader-Meinhoff, and the Venezuelan Carlos "the Jackal," all of whom used Aden as a transit and financial hub for their global operations. The presence of anti-imperialist and left-wing movements in large numbers led academics and filmmakers to dub South Yemen "the Cuba of the Arab World."

Qahtan al-Shaabi, head of the National Liberation Front and the first president of South Yemen, was overthrown on June 22, 1969 by a hardline Marxist component within the NLF. Shaabi's successor, Muhammad Ali Haytham, lasted less than two years, giving way to Salim Rubayya Ali who moved the country toward a more radical Marxist model and an alliance with communist China and the non-aligned bloc of developing nations. Rubayya Ali was joined by two others to constitute the troika of PDRY politics during the 1970s and early 1980s. Rubayya Ali had a reputation as the most extreme of the senior PDRY leaders and his opponents often labeled him derisively as a "Maoist." This derision stemmed from how impressed Rubayya Ali had been by his state visit to China and how he naively tried to implement the later stages of the Chinese Cultural Revolution in South Yemen, specifically those related to peasant uprisings to seize land and workers seizing factories. The second key politician in the PDRY was Abdul Fattah Ismail, the secretary general of the Marxist NLF. As the movement's leading intellectual he was perhaps the only PDRY politician who actually understood

Marxist ideology beyond some Soviet propaganda talking points. Ismail's intellect was also his weakest trait as he lacked the charismato appeal to the larger masses, preferring instead to speak and write using intellectual jargon that could be understood only by scholars of Karl Marx. Rather than focusing solely on PDRY politics, Ismail remained intent on spreading South Yemen's Marxist ideology to Sana'a, a highly improbable scenario that was likely driven by the fact that he was born in North Yemen and lacked the tribal and familial connections to the South, enjoyed by his political contemporaries. The final member of the PDRY troika was Ali Nasser Muhammad who benefited from loyal tribal support in the northern part of Abyan province. Ali Nasser was and still is a natural politician and a charismatic leader.

In 1978, Salim Rubayya Ali was executed, and the two presidents who followed, Abdul Fattah Ismail (1978–1980) and Ali Nasser Muhammad (1980–1986), aligned South Yemen with Moscow and formed the Yemen Socialist Party (YSP), which continues to play a role in modern Yemeni politics. From 1978 until the 1990 unification, the leader of the PDRY assumed the title of General Secretary of the Yemen Socialist Party, a reflection of the country's affinity with the Soviet Union. After he resigned in 1980, Ismail moved to Moscow for the next five years, ostensibly to undergo medical treatment. The divisions that arose among leading PDRY figures was mainly based on personality and competition for power rather than significant policy or ideological differences. The one exception was Ismail's staunch opposition to the private sector despite the PDRY's alarmingly low productivity in agriculture, manufacturing, and fisheries during the early 1970s. The regime's finances were kept afloat only by the grace of Soviet economic assistance.

On the one hand, the PDRY was a successful post-colonial state that adopted a generous social welfare system, achieved minimal income disparities, rooted out corruption and nepotism, and prevented the spread of radical Islamist organizations. On the other hand, the PDRY relied on violence to achieve its political aims and grew increasingly dependent on the USSR to meet its financial obligations. These two juxtaposing legacies of the PDRY are at the core of the current debate among southerners about their region's future.

Why did the two Yemens not unify after independence?

Although Yemen was only rarely "united" in its history and maintains only a vague popular sentiment of a distinct territorial unit, modern Yemenis from both North and South consider themselves an inherently united people. When volunteers arrived from the South to defend the capital city from the religiously conservative northern tribesmen during the siege of Sana'a in 1968, it seemed as if unity was on the horizon. A combination of foreign pressure, unwilling political leadership, and the emergence of two hugely different post-colonial societies prevented unification efforts in 1968 and again in 1972, following the signing of a unification agreement in Cairo. Although the two Yemens shared similar revolutionary ideologies and both peoples were believed to share ancestry, unification did not occur until 1990.

The primary obstacle standing in the way of unification was the existence of an internationally recognized border dividing North and South Yemen. The first demarcation of the border was made in 1873 as part of an agreement between the Ottoman and British Empires. The northern and southern regions were a reflection of where the Ottomans and the British envisioned the hinterlands of their colonial possessions. The British were based in Aden, while the Ottomans were based in the Red Sea Tihama coastal region. In 1934, the British again signed a treaty that fixed North-South boundaries, this time with Imam Yahya. This formal declaration of British defense and support of the tribes surrounding Aden was later complemented by individual "advisory treaties" signed from 1937 to the 1950s, which formalized allegiance to the British Crown in exchange for Colonial Office subsidies and protection.

On an ideological level, the NLF was a very different organization from the tribal republic in the North. Qahtan al Shaabi, leader of the NLF victory in 1968 and the first prime minister of South Yemen, was an ardent Nasserist and socialist, two factors that influenced the South's principal political party, ideology, and security state. Before withdrawing their last troops from Aden, the British Colonial Office had envisioned a post-independence Federation of South Arabia emerging. They hoped to retain the port of Aden while enjoying the security of an independent hinterland. The federation failed for three main reasons: not all the surrounding tribal sheikhs had embraced the notion of southern unity, the federation was entirely reliant on British support, and the British Labour government pressured colonial authorities into a premature departure, thereby not giving the federation institutions sufficient time to organize. British financial support was replaced in the South with loans and influence from the Soviet bloc and China, in direct contrast to the YAR's increased trade with Western countries and Saudi Arabia, thereby further widening the gap between the two Yemens.

South Yemen was one of the world's poorest, yet fastest growing economies after independence, before the decision to nationalize. The state transformed feudalism and tribalism, both prominent features of North Yemen, into socialism, through universal healthcare, education, and employment (especially for women and Bedouins). The NLF absorbed many members of the Aden Trade Union Congress (ATUC) and the People's Socialist Party (PSP), gaining a near monopoly of the left-wing voices. In contrast, the right-wing elements in Sana'a and anti-communist pressure from Saudi Arabia fomented the 1971–1972 border disputes with the PDRY, creating additional obstacles to an immediate reunion.

Even if the two Yemens could have overcome foreign pressures, ideological differences, and an internationally recognized border, unification would have been exceedingly difficult given the instability of leadership during the 1970s. Multiple assassinations in both countries led to successions of prime ministers with no national strategy beyond retaining power and staying alive. This continuous political uncertainty was not conducive to the development of a unified government and national ideology. It was not until 1990, during the long tenure of Ali Abdullah Saleh, that the union could be effectively implemented.

5

ALI ABDULLAH SALEH'S REGIME, UNIFICATION, AND AL-QAEDA

It is terrible the ignorance of what is going on
And more terrible to recognize
Do you know Sana'a who the secret colonizer is?
Invaders who are not observed while their invading sword is in
  my chest
They may bring tobacco in cigarettes, whose color is tempting
In brutal charities that humanize its rocky face
In the eyelashes of a female . . .
In a teacher's trousers, and under the head cover of the religious
  reciter
In the anti-pregnancy tablets, in a tube of ink
In the freedom from sickness, in the absurdity of the age
In the return of the past colonization, in its modern disguise
In the bottle of whiskey, in the bottle of perfume
They are hidden under my skin, and slip from my hair
And above their faces my face, and under their horses my back
Invaders of today are like plague, hidden but it spreads
Hold the birth of the coming and embroider the miserable presence
It is terrible the ignorance of what is going on
And more terrible to recognize.

—Abdullah al-Baradouni (1929–1999),
"Invasion from Within"

Who was Ali Abdullah Saleh?

Saleh was one of the most gifted orators and skillful politicians in the modern history of Yemen. Echoing the famous words of Imam Ahmad during the 1950s who originally used the analogy of snakes to describe the country's tribal and religious politics, Saleh claimed that he was "dancing on the head of snakes." He often bragged that he was the only one who could keep the country together, a prophetic statement that came to fruition when he resigned in 2011 and Yemeni politics began to unravel. His skill with words was matched only by his penchant for corruption, often at the expense of the country's population, and the size of his patronage network funded by Yemen's oil wealth.

Saleh was born in 1942 in the Bayt al-Ahmar, a village in the small Sanhan tribal territory, a member of the Hashid Tribal Federation then led by Sheikh Abdullah al-Ahmar. When he was still a young child, Saleh's father, a simple village blacksmith, died and Saleh's mother married her brother-in-law Muhammad Saleh, who served as Ali Abdullah's mentor and guardian. Saleh left home as a teenager to join the Mutawakkilite Kingdom's army, rising through the military ranks and even claiming to be one of the heroic defenders of Sana'a during the siege of 1968. His military career led directly into a political one with his appointment as head of security in Ta'iz in 1977, and a few years later he became a surprising appointee to the presidency of the YAR. Few expected the son of a blacksmith from a small inconsequential tribe to rise to prominence and to succeed at holding the position of president for 33 years—one of the longest tenures in the Middle East. The key to Saleh's success was not only his personal tenacity but also the fierce loyalty of his family and close friends and the development of a network of patronage built through rampant corruption and bribery. Ali Muhsin al-Ahmar, his cousin and childhood friend, was by his side from the first moments of his entry into politics and remained with him until the Arab Spring when the issue of succession damaged a lifelong friendship, dragging the country down along with them.

Why was he chosen as president of Yemen?

To put it simply, Saleh was appointed president because no one else wanted the job. Saleh's two previous predecessors had been brutally assassinated, and many Yemenis assumed that Saleh's time as president would also be short-lived. Ibrahim al-Hamdi, a popular favorite, was killed in October 1977 by members of the tribal opposition. His successor Ahmad al-Ghashmi was assassinated in June 1978, an unfortunate victim of a local dispute among PDRY leadership in South Yemen. A mysterious explosive briefcase was handed to al-Ghashmi by an envoy sent on behalf of PDRY president Salim Rubayya Ali, who was himself executed three days later by PDRY political opponents.

Lieutenant Colonel Ali Abdullah Saleh was only 35 in July 1978 when he was appointed president of Yemen, a job that few politicians in Yemen coveted, given the very short life expectancy of former presidents. In the months following the assassination of both al-Ghashmi and Rubayya Ali, the armies of both North and South Yemen massed along the border and numerous threats were made on Saleh's life. It looked as if Saleh would not survive past the end of 1979. When it seemed as if border tensions might escalate into a larger conflict that could imperil the Saudi Kingdom, the United States made a fateful decision to ship tanks and anti-tank missiles to Saleh, thus turning the tide of Yemen's North-South conflict. In the aftermath of the Iranian Revolution that had taken place earlier in 1979, the United States chose to support North Yemen out of concern for Soviet designs on the Middle East beyond the PDRY. The declaration of support for Saleh both saved his presidency and marked the beginning of a roller-coaster relationship with the Americans over the next three decades.

What sparked the 1986 South Yemen civil war?

Salim Rubayya Ali was assassinated three days after al-Ghashmi and was replaced by a pro-Soviet Marxist named Abdul Fattah Ismail, who was one of the co-founders of the NLF in 1963. Ismail formed the Yemen Socialist Party in an effort to align PDRY ideology with that of its Soviet Union benefactors. He fled to Moscow, ostensibly for medical treatment, but returned to South Yemen in 1984 to challenge his successor Ali Nasser Muhammad. The ensuing violence pitted those tribes who were staunch NLF supporters (Lahej, Radfan, Yafai, and Dhali) against the more conservative tribes who had collaborated with the British until their 1967 departure (Dathina, Fadhli, Aulawi, and Audhali).

The 1986 civil war in South Yemen was sparked by a particularly horrific incident on January 13, 1986, when Ali Nasser's bodyguard entered a meeting of the Yemeni Politburo and killed members of the socialist opposition with a machine gun. The ensuing 10 days of fighting were some of the bloodiest ever witnessed in South Arabia with thousands of casualties and tens of millions of dollars in property damage. Even Soviet diplomats and their families were forced to evacuate the violence that did not spare the PDRY's principal benefactor. When the dust settled, Ali Nasser Muhammad had fled to the YAR along with 30,000 supporters and came under the protection of Saleh. Abdul Fateh Ismail was killed during the fighting, leaving the YSP leadership to Ali Salem al-Beidh, one of the party's only senior leaders to have survived the carnage and who remained in South Yemen. Al-Beidh served a central role in the 1990 unification with North Yemen and would also be the instigator of the 1994 civil war. Both Ali Nasser and al-Beidh continue to play important roles in Yemen's southern movements, with both harboring dreams of southern autonomy and prosperity.

How and why did Saleh unite Yemen in 1990?

The 1990 unification of North and South Yemen was not the first time that unification was discussed seriously. Both Imam Yahya and his son Ahmad spoke of Yemeni nationalism and sought to expand their authority to the south either through military conquest or unifying rhetoric. After a brief border war in 1972, the leadership of the YAR and the PDRY signed the Cairo Declaration, making known their intention of unifying Yemen under one flag, one capital, and one government. Over the ensuing 18 years, there were other calls for unification, often derailed by border confrontations, regional insurrections, and foreign opposition to a unified Yemen. The ideological and practical differences were eventually reconciled in 1990, spurred on by the discovery of oil along the north-south border and the impending collapse of the Soviet Union, the principal patron of the PDRY.

Since 1970, the YAR had developed a market-based economy, albeit tightly controlled by the government and hampered by protective trade policies. The PDRY, on the other hand, had adopted a socialist command and control economy that had nationalized private businesses established under the British colonial government. Arable land was confiscated from tribal landowners and redistributed among landless families. Large-scale investment in education, health, and social services produced measured success even while economic ventures in agriculture, fisheries, and the port of Aden fell far short of their goals. When Soviet foreign aid declined along with a sharp reduction in worker remittances during the 1980s, finances in the South were in dire straits as the country was inundated with a ballooning foreign debt equaling 180% of the PDRY's gross domestic product (GDP).

For two decades, North and South Yemen were a microcosm of the Cold War, as the YAR's open-door capital economy was juxtaposed with the PDRY's communist and state-driven economy. The two countries were shaped by different histories and two diametrically opposed trajectories. By the end of the 1980s, however, both had evolved along similar lines, attracting a similar list of regional and global donors. The YAR even went through a period of "semi-nationalization" by introducing a state-dominated economy to match the PDRY. Oil discoveries in the Marib-Shabwa basin along the north-south border also spurred the economic merger of companies that operated in both countries in order to utilize Aden's refinery and port along with the manufacturing infrastructure and labor pool of the North. Unification was further aided by the gradual weakening of both countries ideologically, politically, and economically, finally bridging the decades-long divide.

The failure of the Arab communist model in the PDRY convinced the socialist leadership of the need to unite with a relatively wealthy YAR. The unification deal was sweetened by a generous political settlement presented by Saleh. According to the constitution of the unified Republic of Yemen (ROY), the two countries would distribute power equally between North and South, despite the fact that this division favored southern Yemenis, whose population was significantly less than that of the North. Although they adopted president and vice president titles, Ali Abdullah Saleh and PDRY president Ali Salem al-Beidh were considered co-leaders of a presidential council to be elected by parliament.

Unification was not supported by the unanimous approbation of both countries, however. In the South, portions of the YSP and the PDRY's armed forces opposed unification which they feared would diminish their relative political influence. In the North, several influential conservative, tribal, and Islamic figures opposed unification with the YSP, whom they referred to as a "tiny group of pagans." One voice in particular, that of Sheikh Abdul Majib al-Zindani, a prominent Islahi opposition leader, objected to the ROY constitution's adaptation of Islamic shariah as the "main source" of legal code rather than the "sole source." Islah-YSP tensions would be exacerbated by Islah's strong performance in the 1993 parliamentary elections, at the expense of the YSP.

Why did Saleh support Saddam Hussein during the First Gulf War?

Saudi Arabia and the Gulf Cooperation Council (GCC), or the intergovernmental council of Persian Gulf states (except Iran, Iraq, and Yemen) formed in 1982, have emerged as the 21st-century hegemons of the Arabian Peninsula. Before the GCC became suzerain, however, Iraqi president Saddam Hussein formed an alternative economic bloc known as the Arab Cooperation Council (ACC), a historical reference to the Arab Nationalist movements of the 1960s. In 1989, Yemen, Jordan, and Egypt joined the ACC as a show of support for Saddam Hussein and Iraq's war with Iran during the 1980s. Joining the ACC was also Saleh's response to Saudi designs on Yemeni territory in the Hadramawt, where oil had just been discovered. While there are no documented promises, the theory is that Saddam must have offered Saleh substantial economic aid and support in regaining Yemeni territory along the border with Saudi Arabia. Both Saleh and al-Beidh were under pressure to unify Yemen before the May 1990 ACC summit in Baghdad, where a united country would present a far greater case for economic investment and support from Iraq.

Although a united Yemen certainly made a positive impression at the ACC, the newly formed Republic of Yemen had the misfortune of being a member of the Security Council when Saddam invaded Kuwait on August 2, 1990. Accusing Saudi Arabia of impiety for inviting US troops into the land of Islam's two holiest cities and expressing a preference for an Arab solution to the Iraq-Kuwait crisis, Saleh refused to condemn Saddam's actions, despite pressure from US Secretary of State James A. Baker III. Yemen was joined by only Cuba in voting against UN Resolution 678 authorizing a joint invasion of Iraq. Saudi Arabia retaliated by expelling 800,000 Yemeni laborers, thereby curtailing their lucrative remittances. In line with Saudi reactions, the United States cut off all American aid to Yemen, presenting Saleh with a double act of retribution that constituted a serious economic blow to the newly united country.

What sparked the 1994 civil war?

Without US aid or worker remittances, which had constituted 20% of the country's GDP, Yemen's economy during the early 1990s grew even more reliant on oil income. The return of workers from abroad led to an unemployment rate that topped 35% coupled with a significant increase in the price of food and other staples. Rather than use the Republic of Yemen's (ROY) oil income to subsidize food prices and invest in job-creating economic ventures, Saleh distributed the country's oil wealth among northern tribal leaders, developing a robust patronage network that further solidified his hold on presidential power. In response, southerners protested ROY corruption amid growing disdain for Saleh and the country's northern population.

Ali Salem Al-Beidh, then serving as an embittered vice president of the ROY, pressured Saleh to hold free elections in April 1993, believing that the Yemeni population, and the Shafi'i residents of the Tihama and Ibb regions in particular, would rally behind the Yemen Socialist Party (YSP). Al-Beidh misjudged the popularity of the General People's Congress (GPC), which received 28% of the national vote, earning 123 seats in the 301-member parliament, compared with the YSP, which received only 19% and 56 seats. The Islah Party was a close third with 17% of the national vote, earning it 62 seats. In the North, the YSP also received less support than Islah, the new Islamist party in Yemen that won the popular support of the Tihama and Ibb regions over the YSP. With only 19% of the national vote, the YSP and al-Beidh could no longer justify the 1990 power-sharing agreement. As these were the first democratic elections in the country's history, few could have predicted the outcome.

To protest the election that he had requested, al-Beidh retreated to Aden and began demanding political restitution based on the original unification agreement. The civil war, which began in April 1994 with a tank battle outside Amran, eventually became costly, with southern military units launching Scud missiles at northern cities while Saleh's ground forces fought their way toward Aden. Saleh had the support of nearly the entire international community, with the exception of Saudi Arabia, Oman, and other Gulf countries that feared the growing threat of a united and powerful Yemen along their borders. On July 7, 1994, Saleh's forces captured the port city of Aden, marking the end of the short-lived Democratic Republic of Yemen and sending a generation of southern leadership into exile. Al-Beidh and Ali Nasser Muhammad have both remained active in Yemeni politics from abroad and have been strong advocates of southern autonomy.

What was Saleh's relationship with the Islamists in Yemen?

The Islah Party and other Salafi groups were instrumental in Saleh's 1994 victory against southern secessionists as their fighters aided in the conquest of Aden. Following the end of the war and Saleh's consolidation of power, the Islah Party was given authority to set up Islamic institutes of education throughout the country, in which a Saudi Wahabi version of Salafi Islam would be taught. Salafism, derived from the Arabic word *salafi*, which means "original," represents the religious doctrine of returning to the spiritual purity of the Prophet Muhammad's generation and the founding of Islam. Wahabi doctrine refers to Muhammad Abdul Wahhab, an 18th-century Salafi religious scholar, who allied himself with the al-Saud family and whose teachings have since been propagated around the world by Saudi-financed proselytization. During the 1990s, Wahabi Islam gained in popularity across Yemen as Saudis bankrolled Iman University in Sana'a founded by Abdul Majid al-Zindani, the co-founder of the Islah Party. Iman University was notorious for the number of radicalized alumni who carried out terrorist attacks in Yemen or joined the Taliban in Afghanistan. While graduates joining terrorist organizations garnered the most public attention, it was actually the thousands of other graduates, who were radicalized in Salafi Islam and went on to careers in education, that succeeded in spreading Wahabi religious indoctrination and Saudi soft power throughout the country. Alarmed by the divisive spread of Salafis in Yemen, Saleh eventually targeted their organizations, but Imam University remained open until the Houthis shut it down in 2014.

By 2003, Saleh's GPC had become the preeminent political party in Yemen, reducing the opposition parties of Islah, YSP, and the Nasserists to miniaturized versions of their former selves. Saleh had allied himself with Islah before, during, and immediately after the 1994 civil war as a counterbalance to the political power and influence of the YSP. After the reunification of Yemen and the post-conflict decline of the YSP, Saleh no longer saw a direct benefit in allying with Islah and in offering them ministerial positions in his government. Several Islahis resigned, while others sought the YSP leadership to form an unlikely political alliance between two former adversaries. The YSP-Islah alliance reached its zenith in 2003 when Jarallah Umar, the deputy secretary general of the YSP, was invited to address the Islah Party congress. In a crisis that shocked the Yemeni public, Umar was assassinated in front of thousands of onlookers by a former member of the Islah Party. Although many suspected that Saleh had orchestrated the assassination, it nonethe-less drove a wedge between the two political parties.

In 2005, YSP and Islah reconciled and were joined by the Nasserist Party, the Union of Popular Forces (a party of liberal Zaydi intellectuals), and al-Haqq (a conservative Zaydi party) in forming a united oppositional alliance known as the Joint Meeting Parties (JMP). The newly formed JMP even managed to run an opposition presidential candidate in 2006 when they nominated Faysal bin Shamlan, a former oil minister and member of parliament. Although the results of the election were manipulated, giving Saleh a wide margin of victory, the JMP leadership declared that the real victory was in forcing Saleh to campaign and to address important political issues in a public and open manner.

Are there radical religious groups in Yemen?

Tariq al-Fadhli was al-Qaeda leader Osama bin Laden's deputy who fought alongside the founder of al-Qaeda in Afghanistan during the 1980s. After the war, he returned to Yemen during the 1990s, at the request of bin Laden, along with jihadi veterans of the Afghan wars and founded his own coalition of jihadi fighters. Fadhli resettled in his family home in the Abyan governorate, a region of South Yemen that had a long history of animosity toward the socialist government of the PDRY. When the 1994 civil war broke out, Saleh enlisted the services of Abd al-Majid al-Zindani, a Yemeni cleric who recruited for the Afghan jihad during the 1980s, to issue a *fatwa*, or religious ruling, declaring jihad against al-Beidh and the socialist infidels. With this religious stamp of approval in hand, al-Fadhli led his band of fighters to join in the sacking of Aden. After the war, Saleh granted al-Fadhli an official government position, convincing him to change his stripes and support the Saleh regime, or at least serve as a pawn in the president's efforts to manipulate groups of former jihadists to his benefit.

Not all jihadis followed al-Fadhli in his decision to join Saleh's government. Other Yemeni mujahidin from Afghanistan charted their own path, following the inspiration and decentralized directives of Osama bin Laden. Joining these veterans of Afghanistan were native Yemeni recruits, many of whom were graduates of the radical Salafi religious schools that had grown in number since their first appearance during the 1970s. Nasir al-Wihayshi, a Salafi graduate from the Abyan governorate, traveled to an al-Qaeda training camp in Afghanistan in 1998. There he caught the attention of bin Laden who had an innate trust of Yemenis, owing to his Yemeni and Hadrami heritage. Bin Laden, who was still irate about the continued presence of US forces in Saudi Arabia and the growing presence of the US military in Yemen, entrusted Wihayshi with a senior role in al-Qaeda's branch in Yemen where Saudi Wahabi proselytization had already begun to make inroads in the population. Saleh's regime became an al-Qaeda target as operatives began kidnapping Western tourists, a fact that both embarrassed the government and harmed what was left of Yemen's declining tourism industry. Kidnapping foreigners in Yemen had become a relatively common occurrence in past decades, as tribal leaders used this to pressure Saleh's regime for political concessions. Few foreigners were harmed in the process, with most actually enjoying the tribal hospitality and cultural experience. The relatively benign tribal kidnappings were replaced by al-Qaeda's brutal operations using heavy weaponry in their capture, resulting in a rising number of casualties among tourists from the United States, the United Kingdom, Spain, and South Korea.

Despite the fact that al-Qaeda's footprint continued to expand in Yemen, the US Navy began using Aden in 1999 as a refueling station in an effort to reconcile with Saleh after the Gulf War diplomatic fallout. Nasir al-Bahri and Abd al-Rahim al-Nashiri, two al-Qaeda operatives who had recently returned to Yemen, began planning an attack against one of the growing number of US military ships visiting the port city. On October 12, 2000, the USS *Cole*, a US destroyer under the command of Kirk Lippold, entered the Gulf of Aden for refueling. A small boat laden with explosives and piloted by two al-Qaeda operatives pulled up alongside the USS *Cole* and blew a 40-square foot hole in the side of the ship, crippling the destroyer, killing 17 crew members, and wounding another 39.

The ensuing investigation morphed into an institutional struggle for power as John O'Neil, the lead FBI investigator, sought a more comprehensive inquiry into al-Qaeda's activities, while US Ambassador Barbara Bodine was trying to shield improving US-Yemen relations from the attack's aftermath. The interrogation of detained suspects was overseen by Lebanese-American FBI agent Ali Soufan, whose efforts at uncovering bin Laden's plot to attack the United States were hindered by this bureaucratic infighting. In the weeks immediately after the terrorist attacks on New York and Washington on September 11, 2001, Ali Soufan uncovered direct links between the al-Qaeda cell in Yemen, the attack on the USS *Cole*, and the planning of the September 11 attacks.

When was al-Qaeda of the Arabian Peninsula founded?

President George W. Bush's War on Terror was an economic windfall for Saleh. After investigations revealed a connection between Yemen's al-Qaeda branch and the September 11 attacks, Saleh was given an aid package worth $400 million in exchange for cooperation in hunting down the terrorist organization. Saleh cajoled several tribal leaders into turning in al-Qaeda operatives who had taken shelter in their territory while he used military force to apprehend and kill others. Saleh's anti-terror program proved ineffective on October 6, 2002, when the MV *Limburg*, a French oil tanker, was attacked by al-Qaeda operatives steering a small boat packed with explosives off the coast of al-Mukalla, a port on Yemen's southern coast. Abd al-Rahim al-Nashiri, orchestrator of the USS *Cole* attack, was again at the center of organizing this second demonstration of al-Qaeda's reach in Yemen. The 2002 attack and the increasing audacity of al-Qaeda activity in Yemen led to a major shift in US counterterrorism with the first use of Predator drones in November 2002. Abu Ali al-Harithi, one of the original founders of the al-Qaeda cell in Yemen, was the first victim of a US drone strike, in what was supposed to be a clandestine intervention. Saleh had initially told the media that the terrorists had been killed when explosives being transported had unintentionally detonated. Within days, however, Deputy Secretary of Defense Paul Wolfowitz, in an effort to score political points before midterm elections, divulged the facts of the US drone strike in Yemen, blowing Saleh's cover. The clandestine drone strikes were now an open secret and a military option that has defined the US role in Yemen since 2002. Drone strikes continue to be a point of contention between Yemenis and the US government. Youth activists have taken up the mantle of protest against these drone strikes. For example, American-educated Fare'a al-Muslimi testified before the US Congress in April 2013 about a drone strike on his home village in the Dhammar governorate that killed five civilians. Al-Muslimi, who has since founded the Sana'a Center for Strategic Studies, argued that the drone strikes were spreading anti-Americanism rather than targeting the root causes of extremism.

As long as US aid continued to flow, Saleh continued authorizing the arrest of al-Qaeda affiliates across the country. The overcrowded prisons and the growing public disillusionment with the US War on Terror encouraged Saleh to look for an alternative to perpetual incarcerations. Staged "prison breaks" certainly did occur, but it was the efforts of Hamud al-Hitar, a district court judge, that succeeded in releasing most prisoners. Hitar presented a plan to rehabilitate jihadists through his subjectively inspirational sermons. Seeing him as a path toward freedom, hundreds of prisoners agreed to sign Hitar's pacifist pledge, even as many returned to violent jihadism and traveled to Iraq to fight American occupation forces shortly after release from prison. This rehabilitation program amounted to a ceasefire between Saleh and al-Qaeda as the freed prisoners disavowed aggression against Yemen, while remaining free to attack the United States abroad.

By 2005, it had become clear to foreign observers that Saleh had little interest in seriously fighting al-Qaeda or implementing democratic reforms, a suspicion reinforced by his decision to re-enter the upcoming presidential race even after committing to step down. The level of corruption in the Yemeni government was so rampant that skeptics warned that US aid for Saleh would only end up in his family's Swiss bank accounts. In response, both the World Bank and the United States significantly reduced the amount of aid to Yemen. US officials ominously declared at the end of 2005 that al-Qaeda in Yemen was no longer an issue of concern and that Saleh was no longer a viable partner in counterterrorism. As if in response to the US declaration, there was a massive prison break in Aden in February 2006. The group of 23 escapees included Jamal al-Badawi, who was wanted by the FBI for his role in the USS *Cole* attack and would remain at large until killed by a US drone in January 2019. Around the same time as the prison break, Nasir al-Wihayshi, bin-Laden's former bodyguard, was thrust into the role of heading al-Qaeda in Yemen after the group's leaders had been killed by Yemeni forces.

Wihayshi revitalized al-Qaeda, which grew to include recent escapees and graduates of Hitar's faux rehabilitation program. Al-Qaeda operatives began increasing their attacks against the Yemeni government, again targeting foreigners in order to cripple the country's meager tourism industry. This resurgence culminated with a September 2008 attack on the US embassy in Sana'a. In January 2009, Wihayshi organized a major media appearance to announce the formation of al-Qaeda of the Arabian Peninsula (AQAP), a unification of his Yemen branch and the Saudi branch of al-Qaeda, run by former Guantanamo Bay detainee, Said al-Shihri.

The newly formed AQAP made international news on Christmas Day 2009 when Umar Farouk Abdu Mutallab, a Nigerian graduate student who was radicalized in Yemen, boarded a Northwest Airlines flight from Amsterdam to Detroit with explosives hidden in his underwear. Although the attack failed to bring down the airplane, it did expose the danger of AQAP beyond the borders of Yemen and focused US attention on Yemeni-American preacher Anwar al-Awlaki, who is believed to have inspired and organized the Christmas bombing and other AQAP attacks. When al-Awlaki was killed by a US drone in September 2011, there was an uproar from civil liberties activists challenging President Barack Obama's legal right to authorize extrajudicial killings of US citizens. Al-Awlaki's assassination did little to stem the growth of AQAP, which thereafter began seizing territory in southern Yemen, culminating with the capture of al-Mukalla, the country's fifth largest city, in April 2015. AQAP was driven from al-Mukalla one year later by forces allied with the United Arab Emirates and has since lost most of the territory conquered during its earlier resurgence. The group remains a presence in southern Yemen, often gaining public support more from their ability to offer governing authority amid chaos than for their force of arms.

How did Saleh envision his own succession?

The most vexing question for an autocratic leader of 33 years is that of succession. After more than three decades in power, having accumulated countless accolades and built up a robust patronage network and personal fortune, it is not surprising that Ali Abdullah Saleh was beginning to see his succession in terms of a family dynasty. Even before Saleh was killed in December 2017, the question of his replacement had sparked a political struggle that in many ways had led to the current civil war.

During the early 1990s, General Ali Muhsin al-Ahmar, Saleh's boyhood friend and his most trusted military adviser, was widely seen as his successor. Ali Muhsin played a central role in the 1994 civil war by securing the allegiance of northern tribesmen and rallying the support of jihadis who had recently returned from Afghanistan. Saleh's decision to appoint his son Ahmed Ali as the commander of the Republican Guard and Special Forces led to early rumors of dynastic succession. These rumors were further supported by Saleh's conduct during the six wars against the Houthis (2004–2010). General Ali Muhsin was sent to quell the Houthi rebellion, yet was purposely not given access to new arms procured from Russia or support from the Republican Guards. Additional evidence points to a plot to have Ali Muhsin fall victim to an errant missile during the northern campaign.

Saleh's alliance with the Houthis after 2014 led to more speculation that he had initially spurred the northern rebellion as a way to drive Ali Muhsin out of Sana'a. It seems that Saleh was hoping to build on fears of Ali Muhsin's Islahi political leanings and stir up Zaydi opposition. Analysts conjectured that Saleh's former vice president Mansur Hadi may have also been complicit in the anti-Islah alliance with the Houthis, which may help to explain why he ignored Houthi military expansion in the months leading up to their seizure of Sana'a. This expansion specifically targeted the tribal areas loyal to Sheikh Hamid Abdullah al-Ahmar and his sons, who also presented a military threat to Saleh's plans for succession. While no definitive conclusion can be reached based on limited evidence that can be gleaned from the inner workings of the Saleh regime, there is a general agreement that Saleh's succession politics further inflamed growing tensions within the country, which led to the current civil war. As Yemeni researcher Maysa Shujaa remarked, Saleh's frequently used depiction of his 33-year presidency as a "ticking time bomb" may be far more appropriate than "dancing on the head of snakes" because the bomb will eventually explode killing its maker. Saleh's ticking time bomb of Yemeni politics, corruption, nepotism, and neglect has been exploding gradually over the past 10 years, leaving the next generation of Yemenis to pick up the remaining shards.

6

THE HOUTHI WARS (2004–2010)

I harvested thorns from a tree
  Whose roots I planted with my own hand
They bloodied me and caused me pain,
  Its stinging limbs tore at my body.
It was I who watered it
  And naught but I nourished it.
Nothing of beauty courses through my veins
  When I stand before it; nothing warms my heart.
I alone am responsible for my pain
  Since it was I who misplaced my integrity.[1]

—Muhammad al-Zubayri (1910–1965),
"The Traitor's Seedlings"

Who are the Houthis?

The Houthis are a family that traces its origins to the Bayt Zayd al-Husniyyah family from Huth, a settlement near Khamir in the 'Amran governorate in northern Yemen. Badr al-Din al-Houthi (1926–2010), the family patriarch, relocated to the Sa'dah region during the 1990s and gained prominence as a well-respected *sayyid* and tribal leader, although his family were considered "immigrants" to the area. The Houthi family brought to Sa'dah an extreme religious devotion to self-proclaimed authentic Zaydi principles,

---

1. Muḥammad Maḥmūd al-Zubayrī, *Ṣalāh fī al-jaḥīm*. Sana'a: Dār al-Kalima, 1985. Translated by Sam Liebhaber, 45.

stoking sectarian divisions in a country where they had not previously been a factor.

Badr al-Din's son, Hussein al-Houthi, also became a religious cleric and participated in Yemeni republican politics, later assuming a central position in the anti-Salafi and Zaydi revivalist movement in Yemen's northern regions. Hussein's early charitable efforts included funding projects for school construction, electrification, and water supply in the country's northernmost territories, an area long neglected by Yemen's government. Similar to the social programs undertaken by Hezbollah in Lebanon, these highly visible initiatives garnered the Houthi family a degree of local prestige and legitimacy, rivaling Saleh's waning influence in the broader Sa'dah region.

The movement, posthumously titled "Houthi" after the death of Hussein Badr al-Din al-Houthi in 2004, has evolved into a unifying call of protest for northerners who suffered from unequal distribution of state funds and political power under Saleh. The Yemeni republic had been implementing restrictive policies as part of a concerted effort to politically and socially ostracize the northern population most closely associated with the losing royalist side of the 1960s civil war. From a religious perspective, radical Salafi proselytization, funded in part by the Saudi monarchy, served as a catalyst for al-Houthi's anti-Salafist movement's growth, first as a grassroots Zaydi religious renaissance during the 1990s and eventually growing into a political, social, and military organization over the subsequent two decades.

In the 1990s, Badr al-Din's son Muhammad al-Houthi helped establish Muntada al-Shabab al-Mu'min, or the Assembly of the Believing Youth, as a counter to Salafi religious and social activism that eventually reached 18,000 students in the Sa'dah region and many thousands more in other governorates. Coupled with an organization of Zaydi educational institutions, *madaris 'ilmiyyah*, or scientific schools, founded by Zaydi scholar Muhammad Yahya 'Izzan, these two individuals and their religious organizations constituted the core of the Zaydi religious revival. A unique Zaydi curriculum was developed and incorporated as part of a summer school program for teens from rural areas in northern Yemen, intended to provide them with a social and educational supplement to reinforce their Zaydi identity.

The religious struggle between Zaydis and Salafis manifested itself most noticeably in school and university curricula and in differing ritualistic motions during daily prayers. Salafi preachers added fuel to the doctrinal disputes by openly encouraging their followers to destroy Zaydi gravestones and cemeteries in the great Sa'dah city region, the commemoration and worship of whom was seen as antithetical to traditional Islam. To this religious dimension, one could also add the perceived differences in social class between the two religious groups. The Salafis were financed by wealthy donors from the Gulf States, Saudi Arabia, and Yemen, while the Zaydis were seen as relatively poor locals without the means to compete financially with the growing Salafi network in North Yemen. Salafis also had the benefit of Yemeni military support, especially after the 1998 appointment of Ali Muhsin al-Ahmar, a supporter of Salafis and Islamists in Yemen, to be commander of the Northwestern Region. The Saleh administration ignored Zaydi protestations, thereby perpetuating the image of the Yemeni republic as an enemy of Zaydi Islam. Zaydi political representation failed to secure even a single parliamentary seat in the 1997 elections, leading to the formation of a fringe Houthi movement as an alternative to the prevailing political parties.

Why are the Houthis at war with the Yemeni government?

Underlying the Houthi conflict with the Yemeni republic is a fundamental religious dispute between the historic Zaydi population of Yemen's northern highlands and a republic that has marginalized the *sayyid* families while at the same time adopting the judicial opinions of Yemeni Sunni scholars. The teachings of Muhammad al-Shawkani, a leading 19th-century jurist and reformer who served during the Qasimi Dynasty, have become foundational texts in Yemen. Shawkani was an early opponent of the Zaydi Imam even while occupying a senior government post for the Qasimis. His writings on Islamic thought were an inspiration for the Free Yemen Movement that sparked the 1962 revolution and are an important part of religious education in the broader Sunni scholarly world. Yemeni pride in the products of one of their own scholars is manifested by the extent to which Shawkani's legal opinions have influenced the reform of Yemeni republican law. Shawkani's Traditionist legacy is similar to Saudi Wahabism, a point that Saudis employ in their proselytization and in the spread of their ideology to Salafi institutes like Muqbil al-Wadi'i's Dammaj school. A similar school was established in Sana'a by Muhammad Subhi Hallaq, a Syrian Muslim Brotherhood member who aptly named it the Muhammad bin Ali al-Shawkani Institute.

Following the end of the North Yemen Civil War in 1970, the Yemeni republic adopted an anti-sayyid dimension to the republican ideology. From the perspective of the revolutionary generation in Yemen, traditional Zaydi religious practices and the system of rigid social hierarchy were remnants of the deposed imam. Shawkani's teachings, which constituted an indigenous Salafi tradition in Yemen, were supported by the republic in order to make the imamate obsolete. This government-enforced Salafism transformed an entire generation of Zaydis who grew up without traditional religious holidays and without the strict adherence to Zaydi religious ideology that was closely associated with the existence of an imamate. At the same time, Shawkani and Yemen's Salafist tradition provided the wedge for Saudi Wahabi proselytization and ultimately the Zaydi-Salafi religious conflict at the core of the Houthi conflict with both Saudi Arabia and the Yemeni republican government.

Zaydi opposition to Shawkani ideology and the growing popularity of the Salafi version of Sunni Islam in Yemen spawned the creation of Hizb al-Haqq, or the Party of Truth in 1990. The founder of the party, Sayyid Ahmad bin Muhammad bin Ali al-Shami, an accomplished poet and long-serving ambassador for the YAR, warned that Saudi Arabia threatened the very religious and cultural fabric of Yemen with its Wahabi imperialism. Ali Abdullah Saleh's regime was responsible for having allowed and even encouraged this infiltration from Saudi Arabia to occur. The irony was that, at least during the early 1990s, Saleh supported the Zaydi revivalist movement as a political counterweight to Wahabism and as a way to produce conflict among the government's potential political opponents. Hizb al-Haq ultimately failed to rally popular support, gaining only two parliamentary seats in the 1993 elections and none in 1997. The futility of Zaydi intervention against the spread of Salafism in Yemen eventually led, in part, to the creation of the Houthi Movement.

While the Houthi movement is best known for its religious opposition to the state-adopted Shawkani Salafism and Saudi Wahabi proselytization, it has gradually evolved into a broad-based movement representing those in the Sa'dah region and beyond who have felt economically neglected and politically marginalized by the republican government in Sana'a.

When did this conflict first start and how did it worsen?

The first armed conflict between the Yemeni government and the Houthis began in 2004. There is, however, no consensus as to who bears responsibility for starting the war. The extremist Zaydi revivalist group formed by Hussein al-Houthi, dubbed "the Houthis," continued to gain in popularity as the group's slogan appealed to large segments of North Yemen's population: "Death to America! Death to Israel! Curse upon the Jews and Victory for Islam!" Saleh, who received widespread condemnation for collaborating with the United States in its post-9/11 War on Terror, at the expense of Yemeni lives and autonomy, responded to the Houthi threat by arresting hundreds of their supporters. In retaliation, Houthi supporters withheld taxes from the Saleh's government, cut off the main highway connecting Sa'dah with Sana'a, and occupied government buildings in and around Sa'dah.

The anti-American slogan that has since become the ubiquitous symbol of the Houthi movement was used to great effect during a visit to Sa'dah in early 2004 by US ambassador Edmund Hull, who was accompanied by Saleh, and Islahi members of Parliament 'Abdullah al-Ahmar and Abdul Majid al-Zindani. As the group exited Sa'dah's historic al-Hadi Mosque they were greeted by Houthi followers shouting the slogan. Upon returning to Sana'a, Hull and the US Embassy pressured Saleh to arrest hundreds of Houthi protesters, further galvanizing Hussein al-Houthi's anti-Americanism and drawing lines in the sand between Saleh and his growing Houthi foe to the north. The slogan continued to spread like wildfire through Friday prayers at an increasing number of mosques across northern Yemen, leading to more government arrests, garnished government salaries for Houthi sympathizers, and the closing down of Houthi-sponsored schools.

These final acts of defiance in the presence of the US ambassador convinced Saleh to place a bounty on Hussein al-Houthi's head as he ordered the increasingly popular rebel to appear in Sana'a and turn himself in to the government on April 27, 2004. Hussein refused, sending instead a deceptively respectful letter that excused his absence in Sana'a, yet also reiterated his allegiance to Saleh's state, citing only the Houthi family's duty to defend their national home against the United States and Israel, the two enemies of Islam.

In the weeks that followed, Saleh appointed Brigadier General Ali Muhsin al-Ahmar, a devout Salafi and an opponent of Zaydi revivalism, to oversee the military repression of the Houthi uprising in the North. Ali Muhsin, Saleh's boyhood friend and one of his closest political allies, had also been entrusted with defeating the southern secessionist movement in 1994. Tensions between the two childhood friends had begun to emerge surrounding the question of presidential succession, which Saleh envisioned for his eldest son Ahmad. The Sa'dah Wars were the "poisoned chalice" that Saleh gave Ali Muhsin in an effort to distance him from Sana'a.

The first shots fired by Ali Muhsin's armored division at the Houthi farm near Sa'dah in June 2004 marked the beginning of a six-year civil war that eventually led to the downfall of the entire republic. In what became known as the first Sa'dah War, the military targeted the Marran mountains near Sa'dah using bombers, helicopters, and artillery against the lightly armed Houthi tribesmen, who took cover in their mountainous cave hideouts. An estimated 20,000 troops, which included tribal irregulars from the Hashid Federation, were deployed in the Sa'dah region and placed the city under siege. The death of Hussein al-Houthi, the movement's leader and former political representative in Sana'a, outside his cave hideout on September 10, 2004, may have marked the end of the first battle between the government and the Houthis, but it was also a turning point that transformed the Houthis from a fringe Zaydi revivalist group into a mass movement united behind its martyred leader.

In the weeks following the military defeat of the Houthi movement in September 2004, Saleh targeted Zaydi activists throughout the country, arresting 1,000 alleged Houthi supporters. At the same time, Saleh invited Badr al-Din al-Houthi and Abdullah al-Razzami, Hussein al-Houthi's son-in-law, to Sana'a for negotiations regarding war restitution, amnesty for those recently arrested, and a permanent solution to the government's conflict with the Houthi movement. After two months of virtual house arrest, they left Sana'a without even having secured a private meeting with Saleh. Prior to leaving the city in March 2005, Badr al-Din conducted his first and only public interview with Jamal 'Amir of the newspaper, *al-Wasat*. This widely circulated interview gave the Houthi movement a nationwide stage to portray their rebellion as a "defense of Islam" against a Yemeni government allied with US imperialism. He argued that the republic itself was a poor substitute for the golden era of the Zaydi imamate and the social hierarchy centered around the *sayyid* class.

Saleh was enraged by the interview and authorized a second Sa'dah War to hunt down Badr al-Din and al-Razzami. The Houthi movement, which so easily succumbed to overwhelming military force in the first Sa'dah War, was far better prepared for the second onslaught. After Hussein al-Houthi's death, the movement had coalesced around his brother Abdul Malek al-Houthi, who emerged as a talented battlefield strategist and charismatic leader. Supplemented by increasing numbers of tribal militiamen, Abdul Malek organized a guerilla campaign against the Yemeni army, employing ambushes and hit-and-run tactics on military convoys before fleeing to the mountainous strongholds out of the range of Yemeni airpower and artillery. Saleh's indiscriminate bombing campaign had the effect of uniting the Houthi movement with a larger number of surrounding tribes who were now inclined to ally as a common enemy of Saleh and the Yemeni army. Saleh officially announced an end to the Second Sa'dah War in April 2005, after Abdullah al-Razzami surrendered and tribal authorities mediated between the Houthis and the government.

Fighting did not actually come to an end in April, however, as the Yemeni military maintained a presence in the Sa'dah region and Houthi supporters carried out sabotage attacks against military bases and in the capital city of Sana'a. The third Sa'dah war began in November 2005 when dozens of military units were deployed against Matrah and al-Naq'ah, two mountainous cave strongholds that housed the Houthi leadership. Ground troops failed to penetrate this difficult terrain. The Yemeni military relied on airpower to intimidate Houthi tribesmen who remained untouched within the safety of their natural cave bunkers, reminiscent of Egypt's futile efforts to bomb Imam Muhammad al-Badr's royalist troops during the 1960s. The third Sa'dah war marked the emergence of splinter Houthi groups in the al-Jawf and 'Amran governorates. The Yemeni air force began to target them as well, seeking to stem the tide of sabotage attacks emanating from these regions. At the same time, Houthi prisoners openly rebelled against the wardens of the Qihzah prison in Sa'dah, leading to the death of seven prisoners in December 2005. Prison rebellions, a reaction to Saleh's broken promises of amnesty for Houthi fighters, achieved their greatest public relations success in January 2006 with the well-orchestrated and daring escape of two Houthi field commanders from the Criminal Investigation Prison in Sana'a.

Having failed to achieve its main objectives of eliminating Houthi leadership and bringing down the growing Zaydi revivalist movement, Saleh's government declared a temporary truce in February 2006. Although the upcoming elections in September were the real reason for calling an end to the violence, the lull in fighting did give rise to expectations of a permanent and peaceful resolution. Libya's Muammar Qaddafi was invited by Yahya al-Houthi to mediate between Saleh and the Houthis, something that turned into a media circus as it turned out that Qaddafi was far more interested in enacting a measure of political revenge against Saudi Arabia than leading a genuine peace-building effort. Libya and Yemen both recalled their mutual ambassadors over the diplomatic charade as North Yemen began gearing up for a fourth round of fighting.

How did the Houthi wars with the Yemeni government finally come to a resolution?

Even before the fourth Sa'dah war began in February 2007, the local war between the government and the Houthis was transformed into an international conflict. Qatar emerged as a central player in international mediation efforts at the behest of the United States, whose leaders believed that Saleh's continued war with the Houthis would divert resources from the war against al-Qaeda in Yemen's eastern and southern regions. At the same time, Iran and Saudi Arabia began to take a closer look at events in Yemen that were being portrayed by international media as the new front of the regional Sunni-Shi'i conflict.

The fourth Sa'dah war was precipitated by the departure of the Jewish population of al-Salim, located several miles south of Sa'dah. After receiving a threatening letter from the Houthi regional commander, the Jewish community was evacuated to Sana'a and placed under government protection in the Tourist City complex, where they were housed in several apartments overlooking the US Embassy. Whether these threats would have led to violence is unclear, but there is no denying the fear experienced by a small Jewish community upon hearing tens of thousands of Houthi supporters chanting the slogan "a Curse upon the Jews." This incident garnered international condemnation of the Houthi rebels and approbation to Saleh for acting as the guardian of Yemen's Jewish minority. The onset of a new round of hostilities in February 2007 was undertaken under the guise of protecting Yemen's remaining Jewish population of several hundred, suggesting that the entire expulsion episode was a Saleh-manufactured catalyst to restart the war against the Houthis. In June 2007, after two months of Qatari mediation, Saleh and the Houthis signed a ceasefire known as the "First Doha Agreement."

The first Doha agreement offered a path toward reconciliation, but could not manage to foster a trust between the Yemeni military and the Houthi leadership. Even Houthi withdrawals from conquered territory were considered by Saleh's military commanders as nothing more than temporary regrouping before a renewed offensive. This was partially because it was exceedingly difficult to "disarm" a non-traditional army and to force the "withdrawal" of a native population. This first round of mediation came to an official end when a convoy of Qatari representatives was attacked in July 2007 and the Qatari Embassy announced its subsequent withdrawal from Yemen.

The first Doha agreement collapsed in December 2007 after the attempted assassination of Yasir Mujalli, the GPC chairman of the Sahar district, who was on his way to Sa'dah. Yahya al-Houthi, Abul Malek's brother who was in exile in Germany during the six Houthi wars, acted as the Houthi representative in Doha to negotiate a second iteration of the Doha Agreement, which was signed in February 2008. The continuation of violence, however, led to a similar collapse of the second agreement and renewed hostilities resulting in the fifth Sa'dah war which officially began in May 2008. In response to well-organized Houthi attacks on northern government installations, including the airport, Saleh decided for the first time to send reinforcements from his well-trained and equipped Republic Guards whom he had deliberately excluded from previous Houthi wars, preferring to place sole responsibility on the shoulders of Ali Muhsin. Much of the fighting in this round focused on the al-Jawf governorate, Yemen's poorest and most remote regions, where the Houthi message of Zaydi revivalism was reaching a mass audience of potential tribal supporters. The fifth Sa'dah war came to an abrupt end on July 17, 2008, when Saleh announced a unilateral ceasefire in celebration of the 30th anniversary of his presidency. This decision may have been encouraged by international pressure regarding the humanitarian crisis in Sa'dah or may have been a cover for Saleh to remove his beleaguered Republic Guard without additional losses before the planned parliamentary elections in April 2009. Regardless of the actual reason, this unnegotiated end to the fifth Sa'dah war led to 13 months of small-scale confrontations along the frontlines, all leading toward a final confrontation.

On August 11, 2009, Yemen announced the beginning of the sixth and last Sa'dah war, which they termed Operation Scorched Earth. The official onset of the war had been brought about by increasing Saudi intervention in al-Jawf, a region along Saudi Arabia's southern border. Houthi threats against Saudi territory and their continued occupation of the vital Sana'a-Sa'dah road spurred Saleh to make this renewed declaration of war. As the war's title connotes, the Yemeni military was given instructions to destroy any military or civilian infrastructure that could potentially support the Houthis, a direct violation of the Geneva Convention of warfare. What was originally supposed to be a swift two-week campaign aimed at crushing the Houthi movement in a destructive blow, was dragged out until February 2010, as the military failed to achieve decisive battlefield victories. Indiscriminate bombing of large areas of northern territory as part of a collective punishment of the entire population served to further damage republican credibility and drive additional segments of the population into the Houthi camp.

When Saudi Arabia intervened militarily against the Houthis in November 2009, it placed pressure on the movement's leadership to seek a political resolution. Saleh was as desperate to avoid losing this war as Abdul Malek al-Houthi was intent on avoiding a two-front war against Saleh and Saudi Arabia simultaneously. The cease-fire in February 2010 may have officially ended the Sa'dah wars, but it included no written and signed agreements on which further reconciliation could be negotiated. Qatari mediators hosted the signing of the Third Doha Agreement on June 27, 2010. It was based on a six-point plan proposed by Saleh for a cessation of Houthi violence against Saudi Arabia, a withdrawal from government buildings and highways, and the release of all prisoners. The sixth war ended with Houthi militias having retained strategic positions in al-Jawf and on the border with Ma'rib, setting the stage for the Houthi conquest of Sana'a four years later. As a fitting end to the Sa'dah wars, the Houthi movement adopted the religiously inspired title of Ansar Allah, or the Partisans of God.

The end of the Sa'dah wars did not mean the end of fighting in North Yemen or the cessation of Houthi hostility toward the Yemeni government. In December 2010, dual suicide bombings orchestrated by AQAP targeted Houthi religious processions in al-Jawf and Sa'dah under the banner of "Operations in Defense of Ahl al-Sunnah." This new confrontation between AQAP and the Houthis was seen as both a manifestation of the collaboration between Saleh and al-Qaeda elements in Yemen and a harbinger of the anti-Salafi military campaigns that the Houthi movement would begin launching in the subsequent years.

Are the Houthis allied with Iran?

Hussein al-Houthi, the political founder of the Houthi movement, traveled to Khartoum, Sudan, for an MA degree in Quranic studies in 1999, returning to Sa'dah with newfound radical religious beliefs. In 2001, he dubbed his followers Ashab al-shi'ar, or the Followers of the Slogan, which has now become the infamous symbol of the movement: al-Mawt li-Amrika, al-Mawt li-Isra'il, al-la'nah 'ala al-yahud, al-nasr li-islam, or "Death to America, Death to Israel, a Curse upon the Jews, Victory for Islam." This slogan was directed against the US global War on Terror and specifically targeted Saleh's post-9/11 alliance with President George W. Bush. As opposition to the US invasion of Iraq spread across the Middle East, Hussein al-Houthi's choice of slogan became even more prescient. It was a ubiquitous call to arms that went beyond the borders of northern Yemen and beyond the local sectarian, social, and economic grievances that first spawned the Zaydi revivalist movement.

Hussein al-Houthi's pan-Islamic appeal emulated the ideology and model of resistance used by the Iranian revolution and by Lebanon's Hezbollah, even adopting a signature Iranian political slogan for use in Yemen. Badr al-Din al-Houthi, the father of Hussein and Abdul Malek, spent a brief political exile in Iran during the 1990s, after the establishment of the Zaydi Hizb al-Haqq party earned the ire of the Saleh government. Badr al-Din's time in Iran introduced him to the radical political thought that characterized the Islamic Revolution, a political ideology built upon social justice, liberation, and resistance to the West, tenets that found a receptive audience in the underdeveloped and neglected northern regions of Yemen. This apparent Iranian connection fueled local suspicions espoused by non-Houthi Zaydis, that the entire movement was not a return to authentic Zaydi Islam but was rather borrowing doctrine from Iranian twelver Shi'ism. Young Zaydis, in particular, had never lived under the rule of a Zaydi imam and instead came of age in a republic that barred traditional Shi'i holidays and religious practices. The resuscitation of these holidays by the Houthi movement must have seemed like religious imperialism. Although Badr al-Din al-Houthi did not openly advocate the return of the imamate, young Yemenis saw the family's sayyid status and the movement's praise for the era of Zaydi imams as a challenge to the country's democratic development and modernization. In truth, the Houthi political position remains based on an understanding that sayyid rule is recommended and a Zaydi imamate is the ideal form of government, although a religiously inspired republic is considered acceptable—something that is certainly based on the Iranian model of Vilayet al-Fakih, or Guardianship of the Islamic Jurist.

Ali Abdullah Saleh used Houthi rhetoric and early suspicions of their Iranian influence as justification for his decision to incorporate his struggle against the northern Houthi movement within his role in the Global War on Terror. Hussein al-Houthi's anti-imperialist and anti-American slogan both served to galvanize his followers, but it also gave Saleh an excuse to target the grassroots movement that had originally been founded on claims of discrimination and the absence of social justice toward the country's Zaydi population. The slogan spread like wildfire across northern mosques, even without the personal encouragement of Hussein al-Houthi. He had created a self-perpetuating popular chant that embodied the frustrations of both Zaydis and the Arab world in general.

During the six Sa'dah wars from 2004 to 2010, Saleh reiterated his accusations that Iran was actively supporting the Houthi rebels. Such accusations, based only on tenuous evidence, were particularly valuable for Saleh's regime, as it pressured Saudi Arabia to intervene and support Saleh's war against the Houthis with financial backing for Yemen's armed forces and even direct military intervention in 2009. Hussein al-Houthi's successful slogan of "Death to America, Death to Israel . . ." was both a posthumous rallying call for the Houthi movement and a costly liability as Saleh used the movement's anti-American stance as leverage in securing US budgetary and military support for Yemen.

In reality, the Houthi movement warranted little Iranian attention prior to Saudi intervention in 2009, at which point the number of arms shipments from Iran to Yemen may have increased, although no incontrovertible evidence of this fact has been presented. After the Houthis seized Sana'a in 2014, Iranian representatives began assisting the Houthi movement more openly. There are several dozen reported Iranian advisers in Sana'a in 2020 and likely some clandestine shipment of arms and money regularly arriving in Yemen from Iranian sources. When compared with the thousands of bombs dropped by Saudi Arabia at the behest of the internationally recognized Yemeni government, the Iranian contribution seems relatively minor. What is evident in viewing the history of the Houthi conflict beginning in 2004 is that Saleh's accusations of Iranian machinations in Yemen became a self-fulfilling prophecy.

What was the state of Saudi-Yemeni relations prior to the Houthi conflict?

Cross-border smuggling, drug trafficking, and illegal immigration are often topics discussed at great length when referring to the US southern border with Mexico. While only half the length, the Saudi-Yemeni border of 1,458 km has many of the same issues, as drugs, migrants, weapons, anti-American propaganda, and extremist religious ideology continue to cross this permeable border.

Border issues between Yemen and Saudi Arabia began in 1932 shortly after the founding of Saudi Arabia. Abdul Aziz Al Saud sent emissaries to the Yemeni Imam Yahya in an effort to resolve a border dispute between the two countries. Failed negotiations led to a war in 1933 during which Yahya and his northern tribal allies were soundly defeated and forced to cede three disputed provinces along the Saudi-Yemeni border as part of the 1934 Treaty of Taif (see Map 2). The Saudi regions of Asir, Najran, and Jizan, which share direct familial links across the border with Yemen, receive a disproportionately lower share of Saudi oil wealth and political representation, a point of continued contention between the two countries. The original 1934 treaty allowed for a 20 km common border area, specifically intended for border residents to traverse freely. It was reaffirmed in 1953 and 1973 but became a point of contention in 1990 when the united Republic of Yemen resuscitated its claims on the disputed northwestern territories. The two countries nearly came to arms between 1990 and 1994 as border tensions escalated amid Saudi Arabia's conflict with Iraq and the 1994 civil war in Yemen. Syria and the United States intervened to broker a delay in the final resolution of national borders while avoiding violence in the short term. In 1998, tensions again escalated to the point of armed conflict over ownership of al-Durwymah, a small island in the Red Sea.

Over seven decades, Saudi southern border strategy incorporated borderland tribal leaders into the royal family's patronage network and even supported the deposed imam Muhammad al-Badr and his northern followers in 1962 as a buffer to massing Egyptian troops in Middle Yemen. A continued policy of regular payments to Yemeni tribes and relatively lax border control was not sustainable, as weapons smuggling, human trafficking, and the growing threat of regional terrorists made this southern border a domestic security liability. In 2000, Yemen and Saudi Arabia concluded the Treaty of Jeddah officially demarcating the border and recognizing Saudi sovereignty over the three regions. Yemeni president Ali Abdullah Saleh was convinced to relinquish his country's claims to the border provinces by receiving in exchange swaths of territory in the eastern desert regions and by being offered Yemeni membership in the Gulf Cooperation Council (GCC). Saleh's palms were further greased by

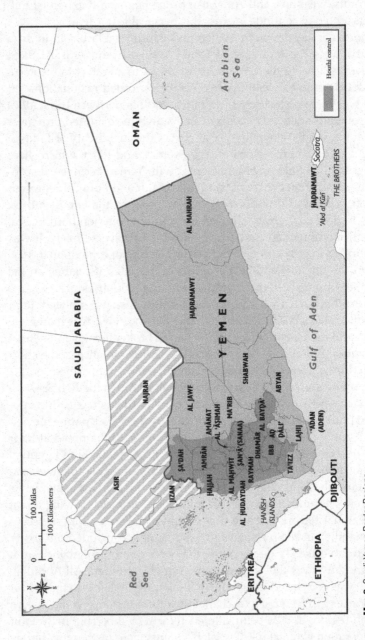

Map 2 Saudi-Yemen Border Regions

a reduction in Yemen's debt to Saudi Arabia and a new $350 million loan for development. There were also speculations that the border regions in each state contained oil resources, and the leaders of both countries were eager to secure a peaceful resolution so that exploration could begin.

With this agreement in hand, Saudi officials began construction of a physical wall in 2003, in an effort to exercise full control over border crossings and end freedom of movement for borderland tribes. Fierce Yemeni opposition to the wall, culminating in 2009 with Houthi tribesmen crossing into Najran during clashes with Saudi troops, have temporarily put the border construction on hold, although the Saudis have full intentions to restart construction as part of a general settlement of the current conflict. Houthi seizure in 2011 of the Sa'dah governorate and the subsequent expansion of Zaydi-Shi'ite influence has led to Saudi fears of further expansion into Asir, Najran, and Jizan. Tribal sheikhs, now in alliance with the Houthi movement, were previously recipients of Saudi Arabia's regular subsidies, thereby throwing the entire Saudi borderland patronage system into turmoil. In 2013, the Saudis announced the recommencement of border wall construction and the creation of a newly equipped border police force to prevent cross-border smuggling. The border fence and new security measures were a violation of previous Saudi agreements allowing for borderland commerce and travel. Saudi border policies continue to serve as a source of great consternation for tribes in the area, fueling the anti-Saudi sentiments of the northern regions currently under the hegemony of the Houthi movement.

When did Saudi Arabia become involved in the Houthi wars?

Saudi Arabia did not become directly involved in the Houthi wars until November 2009 when the Saudi air force conducted its own air campaign in support of Saudi ground forces against Houthi sites along the border. Conflicts in Yemen have long threatened to spill over the Saudi border, much as they did during the 1960s civil war, when Imam al-Badr's royalist tribesmen used Saudi territory as a staging ground for a guerilla war against Egypt. Once Houthi tribesmen began infiltrating Saudi territory at Jabal Dukhan, it became clear that Saleh's forces had lost control of the northern territory. Saudi Border Guards were first called upon to combat these border incursions, but eventually the Saudi air force needed to intervene with targeted airstrikes and the establishment of a buffer zone between the two countries. The Royal Saudi Navy also began a naval blockade of the North Yemeni port of Midi in order to intercept arms shipments. Both the aerial campaign and the blockade of November 2009 were precursors of Saudi Arabia's 2015 Operation Decisive Storm.

Houthi incursions continued unabated as Saudi Border Guards proved insufficient and ineffectual in actual combat, suffering dozens of casualties, and leading to a public relations disaster that continues to deter a Saudi ground invasion of northern Yemen in the current conflict. In 2009, an estimated 15,000 Saudi residents along the border were forcibly evacuated as the Kingdom launched its largest land invasion force since the First Gulf War. Jordan sent several hundred troops in defense of Saudi Arabia from the "Shi'i threat" in Yemen. While Saudi intervention certainly pressured Abdul Malek al-Houthi to seek a political solution rather than be forced to contend with a two-front war, it also spurred Iran to reconsider its low level of interest in the Houthi movement, thereby escalating a border security concern into a regional conflagration.

7

AGRICULTURE AND ECONOMY

What have the Yemenis but moments of misery and words of pain
Illiteracy, diseases, great injustice, famine, fear and the Imam
—Muhammad al-Zubayri (1919–1965), national poet and
leader of Yemen's 1962 revolution

Does Yemen have oil?

Yemen was a latecomer to the Arabian oil market, as significant reserves were discovered only in 1986 by the Hunt Oil Company. Contracts between Yemen and foreign oil companies began as a production-sharing agreement that gradually allotted the government a greater share of oil revenue as initial investment was recouped. These agreements were lucrative for Yemeni president Ali Abdullah Saleh's administration as, prior to the current conflict, the oil sector represented 90% of Yemen's exports and accounted for 70% of government revenue. Nonetheless, Yemen ranks as number 32 among the world's oil exporters, with a market share of only 0.7% and with no known prospects of finding additional large oil deposits (see Map 3).

The discovery of oil was one of the main factors that facilitated the union between North and South Yemen in 1990. Most of the oil reserves were located along the north-south border and in the Masila region of Hadramawt. Oil resources peaked at 450,000 barrels per day in 2001. In contrast, at that time Saudi Arabia was producing 12 million barrels a day. Revenue from declining oil sales after 2001 continued to constitute one-third of Yemen's economy while

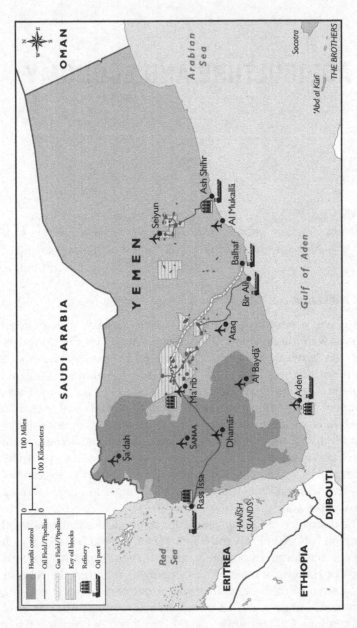

Map 3 Yemen Oil and Airport Map

prices remained high, reaching a peak of $140 per barrel. Following the global financial crisis of 2008, however, when the price of oil plummeted, the government faced a major crisis as the oil price was coupled with a concurrent reduction in production to 250,000 barrels per day. The same cost of production agreements that had lined the coffers of Ali Abdullah Saleh and his regime during the rise in oil prices now became a further drain on oil profits as a larger percentage of the declining output needed to be allotted toward recovering the costs of exploration and production, reducing the profit margins significantly.

Plans for a new liquified natural gas plant in Balfhaf along the southern coast were put on hold at the outset of the current conflict but remain one area where Yemen might continue to exploit this natural resource for export. According to a 2009 World Bank report, in the best-case scenario, the Yemeni government could earn around $10.8 billion in royalties and taxes from the planned liquified natural gas project over a 20-year period. This estimate assumed that obstacles of human capacity and technical issues could be overcome and that the consumer base and market price would at the very least remain steady. Events since 2014 have placed additional obstacles in the way of this project, leading skeptics to doubt whether it will ever come to fruition. The resource curse, however, has negatively impacted the Yemeni economy as the government largely failed to develop alternative sources of income, instead relying on a finite and unstable resource.

What are the country's main exports, aside from oil?

In the years following the oil boom of the 1970s, the chief Yemeni export was labor, primarily to oil fields and construction projects in Saudi Arabia and the Emirates. Worker remittances from Yemen's oil-rich neighbors transformed Yemen's subsistence economy, essentially creating a semi-rentier state dependent on revenues from a finite natural resource. Saudi Arabia had instituted a *kafala* system in the beginning of the 1960s that required every foreign guest-worker to have a Saudi sponsor who would act as an intermediary between the foreigner and the monarchy. Yemeni migrant workers were in a unique situation when compared with their counterparts from

India, Southeast Asia, Egypt, Sudan, or the Palestinian Territories as Yemenis received special status from the Saudi government. Not only were Yemenis not required to seek a Saudi sponsor, but they were allowed to legally open their own business, retaining their family name and company ownership. In perhaps the most well-known example, Muhammad bin Laden made his fortune in this manner, starting as a mason who had emigrated from Hadramawt, and thirty years later he was the owner of the largest construction company in Saudi Arabia—the Saudi Bin Laden Group. The *hajj*, or religious pilgrimage to Mecca, was another legal route for workers; after making the pilgrimage, Yemenis could work in Saudi Arabia for a period of several months before returning home.

Yemeni development was financed by the oil boom, as more than 30% of Yemen's male workforce migrated to Saudi Arabia in search of employment, sending back $1.3 billion annually in remittances by the end of the 1970s, roughly 40% of the YAR Gross National Product and 44% of the PDRY GNP. Back in Yemen, the ensuing labor shortage became so severe that the government had to temporarily ban emigration and withhold passports for those traveling to Saudi Arabia. The growing amount of remittances was not a uniformly positive contributor to the economy as it led to widespread destabilization of local production caused by the import of cheap foodstuffs and manufactured goods. Emigrant purchasing power also inflated the urban property market and increased the price of domestic labor.

The remittance boom, however, was short-lived, as a drop in oil prices during the 1980s translated into declining remittances and fewer incentives for labor migration. Yemeni labor migration to Saudi Arabia came to an abrupt halt in 1991, following the decision by Yemen's UN delegation to support Saddam Hussein's invasion of Kuwait. In retaliation, 800,000 Yemeni workers were expelled from Saudi Arabia and neighboring Gulf states, transforming a temporary labor shortage into a serious unemployment problem for Yemen.

Yemen currently has one of the youngest populations in the world with 60% of its citizens under the age of 25. The high rates of unemployment are even worse for this young population with a rate of over 29% before the onset of the 2014 conflict. Child labor laws are often ignored in rural areas, leading to an even larger labor pool and to the creation of additional vulnerable social groups. The ban on Yemeni migrant workers in Saudi Arabia was unofficially lifted in the years following the Gulf War, but the number of migratory Yemeni workers has not increased to the pre-1990 numbers. Migrants from India, Pakistan, Bangladesh, Indonesia, and the Philippines have since far surpassed Yemenis in both the number and relative percentage of foreign workers in Saudi Arabia.

Aside from labor, agricultural products were the next most lucrative export, but shortages of water and political instability have curtailed some of the largest farming ventures. Since the 2018 publication of *Monk of Mokha*, a popular account of the contemporary coffee trade in Yemen by Dave Eggers, a growing number of coffee connoisseurs have become enamored by the thought of drinking authentic coffee from the birthplace of coffee. Yemenis do not use their coffee beans in any way that would be recognized as coffee by Westeners; rather, they consume the shell of the coffee bean by grinding it into a powder and then mixing in cloves, sugar, and cinnamon in a hot drink known as *qishr*. The coffee bean itself is ground and exported to a limited number of Western markets. Annual coffee bean production had increased from 5,000 tons in 1961 to over 20,000 tons in 2014. Yemen's coffee market, which was on the cusp of revitalization just as the current conflict began, has since ground to a halt in the face of the Saudi campaign of bombing and blockades. Nespresso's 2020 release of an exclusive edition of Yemeni coffee represents some hope for a recovery in the country's coffee export industry after the war is over.

What is qat?

Qat, or *Catha edulis*, is a flowering plant native to the Horn of Africa and the Arabian Peninsula. Citing its psychoactive stimulant properties, most Western and Arab countries have designated qat an illegal drug. In Yemen, Somalia, Ethiopia, and Kenya, qat is widely consumed and has pervaded nearly every aspect of social life from wedding celebrations to official ministerial meetings.

A bulge of masticated leaves can be discerned in the cheek of nearly every person photographed in Yemen—a recent phenomenon dating back to the 1970s. In a country historically characterized by subsistence farming, periodic famines, and a dearth of interregional transportation, qat chewing was limited to a small stratum of wealthy Yemenis. Consumption rates changed as internationally financed roads allowed the efficient movement of goods across the country, and increased worker remittances from the oil boom fueled a new consumer culture. Qat, which had previously been an indication of social status, could now be purchased by common Yemenis in local markets supplied by way of a growing number of paved roads connecting commercial and agricultural centers.

Qat, known for its drought resistance, covers at least 12% of arable land in Yemen and qat growing employs nearly half of Yemen's agricultural workers (about 4 million people). Among Yemen's male population over the age of 12, 72% chew qat regularly, spending up to 10% of their household income on its purchase. As qat represents 6% of Yemen's GDP, the political control of this cash crop remains one of the best-organized and tightly controlled sectors of Yemen's economy, ensuring regular qat deliveries even across contentious battle lines and to remote desert outposts.

Qat cultivation has gradually replaced other crops such as fruits and vegetables, and food staples such as sorghum and wheat, leading to an unsustainable reliance on food imports. Qat is simultaneously a significant contributor to poverty, malnutrition, and political corruption while serving as a substantial source of tax revenue. Local tribal sheikhs, including those currently affiliated with the Houthi Movement, use both the legal and the illegal sale of qat to finance heavy weapons purchases, which translate into political power and security for major qat producers and merchants. Anti-qat public campaigns and legislation, such as a 2002 law prohibiting qat chewing in government facilities, have served only to placate the demands of international donors and have done little to limit its cultivation and consumption. The lethargy and depression brought on by the drug has led to decreased labor productivity and workdays that often end in the early afternoon. Numerous studies have emerged detailing the long-term health risks of qat chewing, including the increased risk of cardiovascular disease, extreme tooth decay, and the danger of chewing while pregnant.

As a social drug, qat provides a psychological escape from poverty, hunger, and violence and helps facilitate political discussion and mediation of tribal disputes. According to political scientist Lisa Wedeen, chewing qat, often in a common lounging area known as a *mafraj*, serves as a forum for democratic dialogue and equal participation because such gatherings are open to virtually anyone who wants to participate, even when hosted by senior government officials. Peer Gatter, a researcher of qat in Yemen, explains that the shrub is not a narcotic drug, but a "mild social stimulant" that serves both as a social evil and as an inseparable foundation of social and political life.

> Qat is a Devil who grew from the earth to devour
>   nutrients of innocent plants.
> Thereafter it trapped the Yemeni man in its seduction.
> Crowding the innocent nutrients in his stomach and
>   flowing in his veins like the Devil.
> It sneaks into his pocket like a thief to steal his money.
> In the morning it chases him to the peaks of mountains.
> And at night deprives him of his sleep, wandering in a
>   maze of imagination.
> It mocks his mind and nerves, bouncing them between
>   happiness and sadness,
> between courageously moving forward and holding back
>   in cowardice,
> between defeat and victory, between wealth and poverty,
>   and between logic and insanity.
>   —Muhammad al-Zubayri, 1958 (the poet of
>   Yemen's revolution)

Why is there a water crisis in Yemen?

In 2012, the World Food Program warned that ten million Yemenis suffer from food insecurity. This number has increased exponentially as the current war continues. Food shortages are not a recent phenomenon but are a product of decades of poor economic and agricultural planning. In a country dependent on rainfall and often subject to debilitating droughts and famines, Yemenis have prided themselves on terrace farming that utilizes the majority of agricultural land to grow sorghum, barley, and coffee, staples of the domestic diet.

Since the third millennium BCE, water harvesting and flood diversion structures helped sustain the country's subsistence agricultural economy, the infrastructure for which was maintained on a local level. Several large irrigation structures were built during times of economic prosperity and a strong central government. The best-known of these was the ancient Marib Dam, which lasted for more than a thousand years before collapsing at the end of the Sabean Kingdom, a symbol of the dynasty's undoing.

During the 1970s and 1980s, unregulated private and public well drilling irrigated Yemen's coastal lowlands and upper plateau to support groundwater-dependent agricultural projects. At the same time, the Yemeni government invested in large public and private schemes supported by USAID and other international organizations. The World Bank, in particular, encouraged water diversion projects overseen by foreign contractors, emphasizing the production of high-value market-oriented crops rather than sustainable and necessary produce for domestic consumption. A demographic explosion during the 1990s, coupled with the return of 800,000 migrant workers from Saudi Arabia and the Gulf, and rising consumer demands for cash crops like qat, have placed unsustainable demands on Yemen's agricultural economy and the water resources of its major urban centers.

Yemen, once known as Arabia Felix for its lush green fields of produce, has now become dependent on international food imports including wheat, rice, and sorghum. City water sources and sewage treatment facilities cannot keep up with the country's rapid urbanization. More than half of Sana'a's water supply, for example, comes from tankers that fill up at wells on the outskirts of the city and make regular deliveries to those households that can afford the cost of a delivered water supply, while others remain reliant on a limited number of public wells. The Ta'iz water system, constructed by USAID during the 1960s and named in memory of John F. Kennedy, has since fallen into disrepair, and attempts at replacement have provided only meager water supplies of very poor quality. The overexploitation of Yemen's water resources through modern irrigation technology has severely depleted ground aquifers and imperiled household water supply to the extent that Sana'a may become the first major global capital to run out of water.

Yemen's water crisis poses a far greater threat to the country's continued existence than the current civil war. Privatization of Yemen's inefficient water and sewage infrastructure can potentially alleviate obstacles related to efficient delivery of and payment for water. Significant price increases would need to be made on non-essential agricultural products like qat and other water-intensive crops in order to cover the higher cost of water. Options, such as large-scale desalination, have been dismissed owing to their prohibitive costs and the challenge of transporting water from the coast to the upper highlands of Sana'a. Seasonal flooding, once seen as a blessing for bountiful crops, has been wasted by severely inadequate state infrastructure that fails to harvest the rainstorms for water supply and groundwater recharge. The famous dams of Marib have not been rebuilt in modern Yemen. Although there are a number of ineffective dams in Yemen all are in need of repair and none are currently supplying significant water to major urban areas or agricultural irrigation.

There are few images more depressing for Yemenis than the massive flooding that has characterized the 2020 rainy season. Rather than a blessing that refills the country's depleted aquifers and reservoirs, the monsoon season has become merely a source of destruction and water-borne bacteria. Yemen's 2008 plan, titled "A Road Map to Harvesting Rainwater in Yemen" proposed the construction of water barriers, small dams, concrete tanks in valleys, and water harvesting cisterns in or on top of houses. Limited technical capacity in Yemen and inadequate funding has stalled the plan, leaving the country's population to watch in alarm as the water table continues sinking. The current water crisis is a culmination of decades of mismanaged public infrastructure and development to the extent that a country in danger of running out of water is suffering from a deluge of water and is tragically unable to capture and store any of it.

Saudis have promised to provide restitution for the destruction wrought by the bombing campaign once the war concludes. Many Yemenis have begun to advocate a Saudi postwar investment in widescale desalination, dam construction, and similar solutions to the water crisis. Others have suggested that postwar reconstruction should seek to diversify the country's economic centers, resettling internally displaced refugees in areas with more abundant water resources. Various other solutions have been proposed, but as yet none have addressed the underlying challenge of transforming Yemeni reluctance to pay for a resource that had previous been owned and administered locally by farming collectives. In fact, qat remains a larger component of Yemeni household expenditure at 10% than water, which takes up only 1% of the household budget. It is clear that the only long-term solution to Yemen's water shortage is a realignment of water rights and sharing agreements that more clearly reflects the needs and resources of the local population. A possible example to emulate is the advanced desalination technology that has recently been developed at a new plant in the city of Ashdod, Israel, that can provide low-cost desalinated water for mass consumption at a palatable level for Yemen's urban centers, thus presenting a possible solution for future consideration. The Middle East Desalination Research Center, based in Oman, was founded in 1996 as part of the Middle East Peace Process, and could play an important role in helping a post-war Yemeni government craft water management solutions to secure the country's future prosperity.

What is the typical Yemeni cuisine?

Hadramis pride themselves on producing what is considered some of the best and most expensive *'asl* or honey in the world. Every major urban marketplace in Yemen has a store dedicated entirely to showcasing a variety of honey from different parts of the country. Each type of honey has a unique flavor and origin, with some cooked with rare fragrant flowers while others were harvested on remote northern mountaintops. Second only to the production of honey is the cultivation of grapes and almonds, both of which are staples of the Yemeni diet. The last Yemeni imam, Muhammad al-Badr, famously subsisted on almonds and raisins while orchestrating a guerilla campaign against the Egyptian army during the 1960s.

Protein consumption varies based on region, with the coastal regions offering bass, halibut, and shrimp from the Red Sea and Gulf of Aden, while lamb and chicken are found in the eastern and southern regions of the country. Each sub-region is known for its native recipes, such as *mandi*, a Hadrami dish of rice and meat cooked in a *tandoor*, a specially designed hole in the ground covered with clay and charcoal that acts as an oven for the suspended meat above. Both fish and meat are flavored with *hawa'ij*, a pungent local spice mix that includes peppercorns, cumin, coriander, cardamom, cloves, and ground turmeric. Hawa'ij use is so ubiquitous that the intoxicating smell pervades every home, street corner, and marketplace in Yemen. The Suq al-Baharat, or spice market, in the old city of Sana'a's main commercial district is an impressive site with a selection of hundreds of spices and mixtures, the purity and quality of which is a source of great pride to Yemenis.

Utensils are reserved for foreign tourists as all Yemeni meals are eaten communally with flat breads or bare hands, obviating the need for forks and spoons. The Yemeni diet is very heavy on grains and carbohydrates that include flat breads or pita, *lakhoukh* (a round and soft spongy bread), *malawach* (fried crispy flat bread), and *jahnun* (rolled flaky dough). These breads are dipped in either tomato sauce or *hilba*, a dish of whipped fenugreek, both of which are flavored with *zchug*, a spicy hot sauce made from red or green hot peppers, garlic, coriander, and cumin. Hilba is the base of many Yemeni dishes, including *saltah*, a lunchtime staple consisting of hilba, onions, garlic, and hawa'ij and often served with lamb, chicken, or vegetables. Chicken or lamb soup, known as *maraq*, is also served with hilba and is eaten using flatbreads rather than large soup spoons. Zchug, hilba, and other staples of the Yemeni diet can be found in specialty grocery sections across the United States and Europe.

No Yemeni meal would be complete with sumptuous desserts consisting mostly of grain and honey-based recipes. The most well-known traditional Yemeni dessert, *Bint al Sahn*, or literally "daughter/beauty of the plate," is a layered honey cake topped with egg yolk and black seeds with honey drizzled on top of the cake as soon as it comes out of the oven. Both Bint al Sahn and *masoub*, a dessert of mashed bananas and bread enriched with butter, cream, honey, and dates, are meant to be enjoyed as a communal meal while sitting around a large plate.

What are the main ports, markets, and banking systems in Yemen?

The southern Yemeni port of Aden was once the second largest port in the world, behind only New York City. It was the center of the

British Empire's thriving Indian Ocean trade and home to a large British Petroleum oil refinery. Instability in North and South Yemen, coupled with the booming oil fortunes of the Gulf monarchies, led to the transfer of mercantile life from Aden to the Saudi port city of Jeddah and the Emirati port city of Dubai.

In addition to Aden, there are major ports at Hodeidah, Mukhalla, and Mokha. The majority of international commerce is conducted through the Hodeidah port, although Aden's Maala Terminal, which opened in 1999, has gradually assumed a more prominent role in trade because of its ability to accommodate large oil tankers and container ships. The southern Ras Isa port, which is used mainly for oil exports, has been the target of Saudi diplomatic efforts to obtain construction rights for a pipeline through Hadramawt leading down to the port. The port of Nishtun in the far eastern region of Yemen, which also receives a small amount of cargo, has gained increasing attention during the conflict for the weapons smuggling within its facilities.

Imports from Hodeidah and Aden are brought to Ta'iz, the country's manufacturing capital, to be processed and packaged and then sent to local markets for sale. Land shipping is by diesel trucks as the country has no rail or more efficient delivery methods for commercial goods. It is very difficult for small businesses and entrepreneurs to invest in alternative transportation systems or any innovative business ventures due to rampant corruption and prohibitive bureaucratic obstacles.

The country's financial service sector and banking system are unable to support Yemen's economic system because of their small size, inefficiency, and rampant corruption that has done very little to engender the trust of local customers. The Central Bank of Yemen oversees 18 banks, with three designated as public development banks: The Yemen Bank for Reconstruction and Development was founded in 1962 to promote industrial development, the Housing Credit Bank was created in 1977 to offer private and commercial mortgages, and the Cooperative and Agricultural Credit Bank was created in 1982 to support the farming and fishing industries, but it has since come to include the growing retail industry.

Financial services are limited both because of Islamic legal restriction on earning interest on a loan and because most Yemenis rely on cash transactions. Although there are personal checking accounts, they are rarely utilized as few trust the banks and would prefer to keep their savings at home. Only a small minority of shops will accept credit cards. The prevalence of a cash-based economy makes accurate statistics and rates of taxation exceedingly difficult to calculate. As only 4% of the population has a bank account, financial institutions have very little capital to finance personal or business loans. In recent years microfinance institutions have been introduced into Yemen, with most administered by NGOs who receive technical assistance from the Social Fund for Development. According to initial studies, microfinancing has greatly benefited segments of the population with no access to a bank or with no credit history. Women, in particular, have benefited from microfinance loans.

Is there any manufacturing in Yemen?

The departure of Yemen's Jewish population in 1949 carried with it the critical mass of the country's artisans and craftsmen. Due to Imam Yahya's protective policies of isolation, Yemen was late in entering a global economy dominated by mass-manufactured goods, an economic revolution that put small local and household manufacturers out of business. The country was late introducing a manufacturing sector. For instance, the Yemeni government waited until oil was discovered in the country to invest capital in the construction of oil refineries, a sector that is in, and will continue to be in, a precipitous decline as oil resources are depleted. Government incentives granted to local manufacturers for import substitution since the 1980s have encouraged private investment, mainly in consumer goods such as food, clothing, and construction materials. The public sector has further supported manufacturing investment in products such as textiles, printing, cement, and petroleum. This small-scale manufacturing provides only limited benefit and employment opportunities. The key to revolutionizing Yemen's manufacturing industry lay in accessing and processing the country's mineral reserves such as gold, platinum, limestone, gypsum, and other ore deposits that can be found in Hajjah, Amran, and Abyan.

To date, Yemen's manufacturing industry has scarcely seen any increase since the 1990s and remains a minuscule portion of the country's GDP. Most of the factories are concentrated around the largest population centers of Sana'a, Ta'iz, and Hodeidah, presenting the fledgling industry with both a regular pool of labor and access to the most robust transportation network in the country. In 2011, Yemen remained ranked as one of the world's least developed countries (186 out of 228). As a result of the Arab Spring protests and the current conflict, those numbers have dropped even further. Coupled with low foreign investment outside of the oil sector before the war and an unemployment rate near 50% for some segments of the population, it may take decades for Yemen to return to even its 2011 levels.

Has Yemen always been this poor?

Centuries ago, Yemen was not only prosperous but was also one of the wealthiest regions of the world. The days of the Arabian spice trade are long gone, and the country may now be the poorest in the Middle East and ranked as one of the poorest in the world, but there is still significant potential for wealth in Yemen. Before the current conflict, more than 40% of Yemenis lived on less than $2 per day, with an average GDP per capita of under $900. Yemen was ranked 154 out of 187 in the UN Development Program's human development index, likely a result of having one of the highest differences between GDP and population growth, which exceeds 3.4% per year—one of the highest in the world. There is some truth to the fact that economic metrics are skewed toward European markets and systems of value, yet it is an inescapable fact that many of the country's resources are underutilized and undervalued. Excessive government regulation, corruption, lack of security, and political instability are the most significant obstacles to economic prosperity.

Surrounded on two sides by warm waters all year round in a nutrient-rich environment, Yemen is endowed with natural fish populations that may rival those of the top fish-exporting countries in Southeast Asia. Despite this potential, fisheries account for only 1% of total GDP, a consequence of insufficient infrastructure, poor management, and a lack of effective marketing and quality control. Transportation options in Yemen are limited as there are only about 14,000 km of paved roads and less than 60,000 km of dirt tracks and trails that can only be traversed with a four-wheel drive vehicle.

The main roads connecting Aden, Ta'iz, Sana'a, and Hodeidah, all constructed during the 1960s and 1970s, are still in good condition and carry the great majority of the country's commerce.

These same waters that supply fish provide Yemen with miles of some of the world's most pristine beaches. While the idea of building major waterfront resorts catering to wealthy American and European tourists may be unrealistic, a small-scale version catering specifically to snow-bound Russian seasonal tourists and local Middle Eastern traffic could reinvigorate declining rates of tourism. Bio-tourism to the island of Soqotra was another idea that had yet to take off before the Arab Spring protests led to a precipitous decline in travel to Yemen.

At less than 100,000 tourists per year before the current conflict, Yemen's tourism industry contributed less than 2% to the country's GDP. This economic sector has been limited by a lack of hospitality infrastructure, a dearth of marketing, and the increasing difficulty of traveling to Yemen. Of the 16 airports in Yemen with paved runways, only five (Sana'a, Aden, Hodeidah, Ta'iz, and al-Rayyan) have international terminals, and all are plagued by flight delays, cancellations, and expensive fares. The high-profile kidnappings of Western tourists did not help to alleviate the perception of a lack of security. Pristine mountains, lovely beaches, and singularly unique flora and fauna on the island of Soqotra could otherwise be a real draw to Western tourists. Similarly, the government preservation of religious, cultural, and historic sites could create valuable tourist attractions for nearby wealthy Gulf travelers and scholars from Western countries. The ongoing renovations of the Aden, Atiq, Ta'iz, Al-Rayyan, Al-Ghaeidha, and Soqotra airports have been put on hold during the current conflict as only the small airport in Say'un is functioning with limited capacity for commercial passenger air travel.

Standing to benefit from an increase in the number of visitors to Yemen is the country's service economy, which constitutes over 20% of GDP. More than half of the service industry is employed by the government or in the fields of transportation and communication. The rest of the service industry, especially in areas of trade, hospitality, and real estate, could experience significant growth if tourism were to increase.

Despite the dire shortages of water resources and the fact that Yemen is currently a net importer of food staples, there remains a great deal of agricultural potential in the country, if managed correctly. There are four ecological zones in Yemen: the Northern Highlands from Sa'dah to Ta'iz (61% of Yemen's farmland), the Eastern Plateau bordering the Hadramawt region (19% of farmland), the Tihama coastal region in the west (10% of farmland), and the southern coastal region surrounding Aden (10% of farmland). More than half of Yemen's cultivated farmland is dependent upon rainfall, while the rest is partially or completely dependent upon irrigation. The agricultural yield gap is extremely high for Yemen, meaning that farmers ideally should be utilizing water and land resources more efficiently and producing significantly more crops. Yemen's agricultural economy has been hampered by outdated planting and harvesting techniques, a meager transportation network, and high prices for water. Already ranked as one of the poorest in water resources, Yemen has an unsustainable gap between water use and water resources, leading experts to warn of a looming water crisis.

Are there any economic prospects where international financial capital could be invested?

Yemen's greatest economic asset is its people. There are nearly 29 million Yemenis and only 4% are over 65, constituting vast potential for a domestic labor force. Postwar reconstruction coupled with government and economic reforms could transform the country into the Arabian Peninsula's industrial center. This lucrative future depends mainly on attracting continued Gulf and Chinese foreign investment and convincing the large numbers of talented expatriate Yemenis to return home or at the very least to invest time and money in absentia.

Yemen's large labor pool could be utilized in the exploitation of several untapped natural resources. Although the amount of available oil is declining, there is evidence of natural gas in significant enough quantities to have warranted the construction of a liquified natural gas plant in Balhaf on Yemen's southern coast. Geological surveys have also located sources of zinc, marble, and granite that have already attracted initial foreign mining and quarrying investments.

Economic reform and expansion are vital policy measures for the Yemeni government that emerges from this conflict, as the two main sources of GDP are no longer viable alternatives. Yemeni worker remittances in 2013 constituted only 10% of GDP, a fraction of the high point during the 1970s. This is a major decline from the 1970s and 1980s, and it is not politically feasible to return to a pre–Gulf War situation, where Yemenis were the preferred laborers for Saudi Arabia and the Gulf countries. In order to be competitive in the international labor market, unskilled Yemeni workers will need to receive training and certifications in specialized fields, an area of recent foreign investment. Saudi Arabia, for example, announced a commitment in 2009 to finance 69 technical training institutes in Yemen. Whether this ambitious plan ever comes to fruition, the Gulf region will need to assist the Yemeni government in finding employment for a Yemeni population that is projected to double by 2030. Oil revenues have continued to decline over the past 10 years, while domestic consumption has increased, thus limiting the amount of oil to be exported for foreign currency. Within a decade, it is estimated that Yemen will need to begin importing oil once again, having exhausted the domestic supply. Finally, the water shortage will have the most significant impact on Yemen, as agriculture remains the largest employer of Yemeni labor.

Perhaps the greatest potential asset in Yemen after its people is the port of Aden. Once a regional hub of commerce, Aden has since declined and fallen into disrepair and disrepute. The city, synonymous with the bombing of the USS *Cole* and the embattled capital of Yemen's government in exile, does not naturally attract the interest of foreign investors, most of whom are probably scared off by the uncertain security situation. A resolution of the current conflict and a measure of stability and predictability could attract much-needed foreign investment to transform Aden once again into the center of Indian Ocean trade as it had been under the British Empire.

8

ARABIAN MINORITIES

Even if the gates of the rich are closed, the gates of heaven will never be closed.

—Shalom Shabazi (1619–1720), the most famous
Yemeni Jewish poet, "Im Nin'alu"

Are there any minorities living in Yemen?

Given the steady stream of news reports of violence in Yemen and the growing problems of internally displaced refugees and a migration crisis in Europe, it may be hard to believe that in 2013 there were still between 600,000 and 800,000 Somali refugees in Yemen. Of them, 85% were unrecognized asylum seekers or undocumented foreigners and consequently outside the purview of the UN Refugee Agency. In addition to the extreme poverty among these African refugees, there is a security concern emanating from lucrative illegal arms smuggling and the flow of extremist recruits accompanying this population movement.

There is a long tradition of migration between the Horn of Africa and Yemen. This cross–Red Sea migration has led to the prevalence of mixed households of Yemenis, Eritreans, Ethiopians, Djiboutians, and Somalis. Known as *muwalladeen*, or the birthed, these groups are subject to covert discrimination by those who do not view them as "pure Yemenis," despite legislation abolishing the country's traditional social hierarchy. During Eritrea's war of secession from Ethiopia (1961–1991), hundreds of thousands of Eritreans arrived in Yemen as refugees. As a result of the war, entire families migrated to Yemen along with African women who gradually came to occupy the economic role of domestic workers, carrying out menial tasks that even lower-class Yemenis were reluctant to perform. Since the end of the war, their numbers have been eclipsed by Somalis and Ethiopians, who now constitute the two largest African national groups in Yemen. Although one can find many excellent Ethiopian restaurants in Sana'a, Yemen's economy is not the main draw for most of these migrants. Many Africans arrive in Yemen intending to cross the country's porous border with Saudi Arabia in search of employment in the oil sector. Most, however, do not succeed in reaching the Gulf oil fields and settle in Yemen for the long term. Undocumented economic refugees from the Horn of Africa, even after two and three generations in Yemen, have no legal status. The Yemeni state and the majority of Yemenis are thoroughly xenophobic and resistant to any formal attempts at integration of immigrants. Without sufficient legal forms of employment, this refugee population has formed its own illegal economy marked by violence and criminal activity, while engaging in piracy, smuggling, and the trafficking of arms and drugs across porous borders.

During the current crisis, ambassadors from Somalia and Ethiopia have asked their refugees to return home as the post–Arab Spring situation in Yemen seemed, to them, far more dangerous than the status quo on the Horn of Africa. Not all migrants were free to return home as some still owed large debts to their smugglers while others were content with their relatively secure jobs in Yemen. Since the Saudis placed a virtual siege on Yemen after 2015, those African migrants who remained despite their government's protestations have become unwitting victims of the current war. Somalis were given refugee status in Yemen and the United Nations High Commissioner for Refugees (UNHCR) has set up camps in Kharaz in South Yemen to accommodate 15,000 refugees. Others have settled in the outskirts of urban areas like Aden and have resorted to begging while suffering from racist marginalization similar to that aimed at the *akhdam*, the darker-skinned minority class in Yemen.

Aside from the African refugees in Yemen, there is a small population of Jews currently living under government protection in Sana'a. Two extended families numbering around 50 persons are all that remain of a Jewish population that was part of the country's social, cultural, and economic fabric for two millennia. This Jewish community is unique precisely because it is one of the only non-Muslim minority communities in the Arabian Peninsula.

When did Jews first come to Yemen?

The debate surrounding the first arrival of Jews to Yemen is hotly contested, both for religious and political reasons. Most Yemeni Muslims believe that the Jewish community shares a common ancestry with the other descendants of Qahtan, the biblical father of South Arabia. Their different religion can be traced back to the Kingdom of Himyar that converted to Judaism during the 4th century CE. For centuries, this myth of common ancestry has served to promote a positive relationship between Jews and Muslims. It has also been used by Zaydi imams as an excuse for policies of forced conversion to Islam, under the justification that they are simply returning the Jews to their rightful ancestral religious origin.

The Jews of Yemen maintain a traditional belief that their community first arrived in Yemen during biblical times, citing an apocryphal story of a tribal contingent that lost its way while wandering the desert with Moses and ended up in South Arabia. The most popular biblical story connects the origins of the Jewish community to an ambassadorial group of merchants sent by the Israelite King Solomon to the Queen of Sheba. Other stories trace the community's origin to the time of the First Temple's destruction in 586 BCE, when a group of 5,000 Israelites, seeing the approach of the Babylonian armies, fled the city of Jerusalem at the behest of the prophet Jeremiah. Upon arriving in Sana'a, this group of refugees believed they had found a replica of the Land of Israel on the peak of Jebal Nuqum, a mountain overlooking the city. There are still stories circulated in the community that claim the caves of Nuqum are a secret passageway to Jerusalem. When Ezra the Scribe issued a call for their return to Israel in 460 BCE, the community spurned his request, earning a litany of curses and condemnations. The importance of these biblical myths is not their accuracy, for none is supported by archeological or written evidence. Rather, they are part of the Yemeni Jewish identity as a people in exile, who would one day return to their homeland, rather than a group destined to remain in Yemen as an inferior social class.

Do Yemeni Jews have any comparatively unique customs?

Shlomo Goitein, the researcher best known for his work on the Cairo Geniza archives, often marveled at the authenticity of the Jewish community in Yemen. Goitein referred specifically to their pronunciation of biblical Hebrew and to their religious customs, whose origins predate the oral law adopted by European and Sephardic Jewry.

Jewish life in Yemen was centered around the capital city of Sana'a, where the central religious figure, known as the *mori*, held his religious court. The mori was often on the road, visiting remote villages in order to rule on questions of *halakha*, or Jewish law. In addition to his religious role, the mori also acted as the community's representative to the imam and the Ottoman governor and as the default tax collector.

Within Yemen, there were four different Jewish sects known as Baladi, Shami, Darda'i, and Adani. Baladi is often considered the most authentic for its strict adherence to traditional religious customs and interpretations. Shami, deriving from the word designating greater Syria, constitutes the largest sect, which has adopted many Sephardic Jewish customs through interaction with Middle Eastern merchants. Darda'i is a splinter sect, originally conceived in the 19th century in opposition to the growing popularity of messianic traditions and mysticism in the larger community. Last, the Adani sect is named for the port city of Aden, where a heterogenous community was home to Jews from multiple countries, who combined their prayer books and religious customs to form a hybrid of religious tradition.

How were the Jews treated by local ruling authorities?

The Jewish community thrived under the 16th-century Ottoman Empire, which provided them with increased opportunities for trade and a degree of social and religious equality. With the rise of the Qasimi dynasty of Zaydi imams in the 17th century came a series of decrees that severely limited the freedom of Yemeni Jews. The imamate's recapture of Sana'a marked a tragic moment for Yemen's minority Jewish community, which was accused of collaborating with the Ottomans and of threatening the rule of the Qasimi

Dynasty. In 1679, Jews were driven from the capital city and other major urban areas in what was known as the Exile of Mawza, to a sparsely populated and dry area in the southern coastal region of Tihama. The location of Mawza was probably intended as a temporary staging ground until the imam could plan for their expulsion from the Arabian Peninsula. This expulsion never occurred, as Imam al-Mahdi Ahmad bin al-Hassan reneged on the original dictate and allowed the Jewish community back into Sana'a. The imam may have realized the prohibitive cost of shipping and resettling an entire population or may have been concerned about the impact of losing the Qasimi dynasty's Jewish silversmiths who ran the country's mint. Although the expulsion was ultimately rescinded and those who survived were allowed to return to their homes, the episode remained etched in the community's memory as the ever-present uncertainty of life as a religious minority in Yemen.

Upon returning to power, the Qasimi imams enacted a number of measures targeting the Jewish community. These included restrictions on the types of clothing permitted, designated areas for walking in a street, and a prohibition against carrying weapons. The most infamous enactment was the Orphan Decree, enacted by Muhammad al-Shawkani, the renowned 18th-century Salafi jurist, which stipulated that Jewish orphans could be forcibly adopted and converted by a local Muslim family upon the death of their parents. Concern about the implementation of this decree led to the widespread practice of child betrothals, as a married girl, however young, was not subject to the orphan decree.

Restrictions on the social life of Yemen's Jewish community did not constitute an immediate danger to the physical safety of its members, as they were under the traditional protective umbrella of *dhimmi*, or non-Muslim status. Security and protected status were offered to Ahl al-Kitaab, or the people of the book, in exchange for a *jizya* tax levied on the Jewish community. Allowances were made for the freedom of religious practice, including the production of wine and distillation of a unique Yemeni version of *arak*, an anise-flavored alcoholic beverage popular in other areas of the Middle East, yet prohibited to observant Muslims.

What role did Jews play in Yemen's economy?

Judeo-Arabic, a dialect of Arabic written in Hebrew script, served as the common language of correspondence between the Jewish merchants of Yemen and their co-religionists in Asia, Europe, the Middle East, and North Africa. This placed Yemeni Jewish merchants and their overseas network at the center of international commerce at the height of Aden's medieval trade and later under the imperial dominance of the Portuguese and Ottoman Empires.

The decline of maritime trade in Aden and Mocha toward the end of the 18th century led to a transformation of Yemen's domestic economy. Having largely abandoned their traditional roles as international merchants, Yemeni Jews gradually trained in craftsmanship and artisanry, an economic sector belittled by the majority Muslim population, who valued the merits of agricultural labor. Intricate filigree silver jewelry made by this community of artisans has come to represent Yemeni artistic tradition. Although silversmiths were the most famous of the craftsmen, and the silversmith families were some of the wealthiest and most respected in Yemen, there were dozens of other crafts carried on by Yemeni Jews, including weaving, blacksmithing, carpentry, masonry, embroidery, and cobblery. By the 19th century, Jewish craftsmen had a monopoly on the country's crafts and artisanry.

The nature of this work and the limited number of consumers in any geographic area led the community to disperse to over 1,000 towns, villages, and neighborhoods across North and South Yemen. At times, individual families would move to remote areas with their craft and unique styles that were passed down from father to son. For example, the cloth produced by the weavers of al-Gades was distinct from the cloth produced in other areas of the country, based not as much on local tradition, but on the particular family that chose to settle in that region. The same is true for the building styles in some cities, with certain designs, such as the Jewish star, attributable to a particular mason or carpentry family. When the great majority of the Jewish population left Yemen between 1949 and 1950, they took their crafts with them, thereby liquidating most of the country's small-scale domestic manufacturing industry overnight.

When and why did the Jews leave Yemen?

The foundation of the State of Israel in 1948 sparked anti-Jewish riots across the Middle East, and Yemen was no exception. Violence began in the streets of Aden in 1947 and sporadically spread northward as news from Palestine began to arrive. Yemen's Jewish community had a long history of messianism and some were ready to declare Israel's founder David Ben-Gurion as the newest 20th-century messiah. Entire communities packed up their families and traveled to the Hashid transit camp outside of Aden, awaiting flights to Israel. In what became known as Operation Magic Carpet, 50,000 Jews were flown out of Yemen by planes and pilots leased from Alaska Airlines and relocated to temporary refugee camps in Israel between 1949 and 1950. The departure was not without incident as local sheikhs demanded high exit fees and even the wealthiest of craftsmen were only partially compensated for property and land left behind. Marauders along the routes robbed the families of what few possessions they did carry with them, leaving those refugees who survived destitute by the time they arrived in Hashid. Nor were the Yemeni Jews completely at ease upon arrival in Israel where they were greeted with implicit racism by a government dominated by Jews of European descent.

Yemeni Jews who came to Israel during this mass migration were not the first to arrive. The strong connection between Yemeni Jewry and the biblical land of Israel, as evidenced by the popular origin myths espoused by the community, served to inspire the emigration of earlier generations of individuals, families, and sometimes entire villages to Palestine, where they formed some of the earliest settlements in Hebron, Jaffa, and Jerusalem. Yemeni Jews even preceded the first *aliyah*, or migration, of Russian Zionists in 1882. After the Ottoman reconquest of North Yemen during the 1870s, the entire empire was open to migration, and obstacles to travel were greatly eased by the absence of borders and the opening of the Suez Canal in 1869. Between 1881 and 1914, several thousand, or 10% of the Jewish population, moved to Palestine, with many fleeing the increasingly punitive decrees enacted by the Qasimi imams.

Given the remoteness of many of the settlements in Yemen, there were thousands of Jews still left behind after the last Alaska Airlines plane departed in September 1950. Communication was always a challenge in Yemen, and additional restrictions had been placed on emigration by Yemeni authorities following the end of Operation Magic Carpet. As the Hashid camp had already been disbanded, responsibility for the remaining Jews who continued to arrive fell on the shoulders of the small remaining Adeni Jewish community. In response, Israel sent a commission led by Max Lapides, a lawyer from the Jewish Agency, to orchestrate the airlift of the remaining refugees to Israel, in addition to the last residents of Aden's wealthy Jewish merchant community who emigrated to the United Kingdom and were given British citizenship. When the civil war broke out in September 1962 and the first Egyptian troops arrived to support the new republic, emigration was placed on hold, as it was no longer safe to cross the North-South border.

Are there any Jews left in Yemen?

Even though the Houthis continue to chant "Curse upon the Jews" at every public meeting, there are still approximately 50 Jews who remain under government protection in the Tourist City compound in Sana'a, upholding the historic tradition of the dhimmi social class. The two extended families in Sana'a still harbor hopes of returning to their homes in the Sa'dah region after the conclusion of the current conflict, a scenario that is increasingly unlikely. These last Jews of Yemen are all that remain of the 4,000 left behind at the start of the civil war in 1962. Those communities that were mostly concentrated around Sana'a, Raydah, and the Sa'dah region lost contact with their friends and family outside of Yemen as they had been stripped of their passports and right of communication by the Yemeni government.

It was not until the early 1980s that contact was reestablished and the plight of Yemen's remaining Jews was brought to the attention of President Bill Clinton of the United States. Yemeni president Ali Abdullah Saleh was pressured to issue passports to this community and grant them the freedom to travel and emigrate. In a campaign led by the Yemeni Jewish community in the United States and supported by Charles Dunbar, the US ambassador to Yemen, all but a few hundred Jews were evacuated to the United States or Israel in what has been dubbed Operation Esther. Additional efforts were made to assist the emigration of the remaining Jews, including a clandestine Israeli effort to evacuate several families in 2017. This is likely the final chapter in the life of a historic Yemeni Jewish community, an Arabian minority that has truly had an impact on the history of Yemen.

Is there still a connection between the Jewish Yemeni diaspora and Yemen?

If one were to ask where the largest diasporic community of Yemenis outside the Arabian Peninsula resides, few would have guessed Israel, which is home to roughly 400,000 Yemenis. Over 70 years, Yemeni Jews in Israel have overcome early decades of racism; they have since reached high levels of political office and have emerged as some of the most successful businessmen, academics, and musicians. There remains a close connection between the Jews of Yemen and their ancestral homeland in their manner of speech, the cuisine of their kitchens, and the qat that is still chewed by the older generation.

Beginning in the 1970s in Israel, a new Mizrahi, or Oriental culture began to emerge that popularized Arab, Greek, and Turkish musical traditions. Most of these Mizrahi musicians were of Yemeni origin and included well-known stars such as Zohar Argov (1955–1987), "Daklon" (Yossi Levi), Avner Gadassi, Ofrah Haza, Zion Golan, and Ḥayim Moshe. The songs of Zion Golan, in particular, have managed to transform traditional *humayni* Yemeni poetry into songs that appeal to modern musical tastes. Golan's music, especially "Sana'a al-Yaman," a tribute to Yemeni culture and traditions, remains enormously popular among Yemeni youth and can be heard regularly on local radio stations. Golan, however, was born and raised by Yemeni immigrants in Israel and has never visited Yemen, as Israelis are officially barred from entering the country.

Ofra Haza, one of the most famous Yemeni-Israeli musicians, known as "The Israeli Madonna," achieved worldwide recognition at the 1983 Eurovision Song Contest. Among her most celebrated songs were those of the famous 16th-century Yemeni Jewish poet Shalom Shabazi as well as other songs in local Yemeni dialect. Her songs gained a great deal of fame in Yemen itself where loyal fans reveled in her ability to beautify local Yemeni dialect through music.

Like Zion Golan, however, she was born to a Yemeni immigrant family in Tel Aviv and had also never visited Yemen, despite the country's centrality in her lyrics and music videos. Abdul Karim al-Iryani, while serving as Yemeni minister of foreign affairs, came to New York City in 1994 to meet with the Yemeni Jewish community, assuming they could help support Yemeni-American relations. Sampson Giat, president of the Yemenite Jewish Federation of America, suggested to Iryani that Yemen follow the recent peace treaties with Egypt and Jordan by opening his country's borders to thousands of Israeli Jews, who either still have family in Yemen or would love to visit the country of their ancestry. Iryani gave this proposal serious consideration and even extended an invitation to Ofra Haza and her family to visit Yemen as his personal guests. On November 4, 1995, Ofra Haza and her family flew to Amman and were scheduled to board a Yemenia Airways flight to Sana'a when news arrived that Israeli prime minister Yitzhak Rabin had been assassinated. The decision was made to return to Israel rather than play at a local concert in Yemen. A second trip to Yemen was never scheduled as Ofra Haza died nearly four years later from AIDS-related pneumonia.

After Zion Golan and Ofra Haza popularized Mizrahi music, particularly Yemeni Arabic songs, many other Israeli musicians and bands have entered the pop culture scene in Israel and Yemen. Yemen Blues, an Israeli band founded in 2010, features the old generation of Yemeni and Yemeni-Jewish songs remixed with a fusion of North and West African music along with Western music traditions like jazz, Blues, and funk. The band's founder Ravid Kahalani (whose family is from Kahalan, one of Yemen's largest tribal federations) grew up in a small Yemeni-Jewish community in Israel. Yemen Blues has performed across the globe with followings in the United States, Europe, Asia, the Middle East in general, and Yemen in particular. Neither Kahalani nor the Israeli members of his band have ever set foot in Yemen, but their music continues to be a direct connection between Israel and Yemen.

In March 2015, the new hit song "Habib Kalbi" (Love of My Heart), based on a mournful Yemeni folk song, was released to great fanfare across the Middle East. The song's music video, featuring three women in full Bedouin Arab dress in a captivating desert setting, has garnered more than 14 million views, with many of the commentators hailing from Yemen. Similar to Kahalani, Golan, and Haza, the three women, Tair, Liron, and Tagel Haim grew up in a small village in southern Israel and have never been to Yemen. Their music is "inspired by the ancient oral history of Yemenite women's chanting," as they grew up in a musical family that prided itself on preserving Yemeni musical traditions. The greatest acclaim for their music came not from within Israel, but throughout the Arab world, where multiple generations of listeners revel at the quality of their Yemeni-dialect and the way they have popularized Yemeni musical traditions.

Shared music, language, and culture have maintained a natural connection between Israeli and Yemeni societies. The popularity of modern Israeli bands and their use of traditional Yemeni dialect transcends national boundaries and political conflicts and creates direct connections with local people. Musicians like Zion Golan, Ofra Haza, Ravid Kahalani, and the Haim sisters have given new life to the Yemeni tradition in Israel, preserving both language and culture for a second, third, and fourth generation of Jews who consider themselves Yemeni, although they have never visited the country.

Are there any other religious minorities in Yemen?

In addition to minority Islamic sects and a dwindling community of Jews, there is also a small number of Bahais and Christians in Yemen. Baha'ism was first introduced in Yemen during the first half of the 19th century by a preacher from Iran named Ali Muhammad al-Shirazi. Numbering around 1,000 followers and scattered among some of Yemen's major cities, Bahais have traditionally been reluctant to declare their religious affiliation in public and have only recently begun holding open community events. Incidents of intolerance and violence have increased in tandem with a growing Iranian presence since 2015, as Iran exported an anti-Bahai hostility to Yemeni society. Under the Houthi government, the continued presence of Bahais in Yemen is under threat as a growing number of religious leaders have been arrested and charged with apostasy, while others live in a constant state of fear.

While Baha'ism in Yemen has a history of less than 180 years, Christianity's presence in the country predates the emergence of

Islam and can be traced back to the missionary activity of Emperor Constantine in the 4th century CE and to 5th-century Byzantine church-building missions in Aden and the Dhofar region, on the Omani border with Yemen. Christian worship, churches, and regular services were maintained in Aden during the British occupation, and several Christian establishments continued to provide services in Aden and Sana'a through 2014. As of 2020, however, owing to the fact that Christians are not free to worship openly in public and remain relatively clandestine, estimates of Christians in Yemen range anywhere from 2,000 to 40,000, which also includes refugees from abroad currently residing in Yemen and Ethiopian immigrants who have been residing in Yemen for several generations. Numerous reports continue to emerge of violence targeting Christian sites and cemeteries over the past two decades, further testament to the very real danger facing the country's religious minorities.

The Yemeni constitution requires that any member of parliament be a committed Muslim, thus barring Bahais, Christians, and Jews from official political participation. Even the National Dialogue Conference in 2013, the post–Arab Spring gathering of all segments of Yemeni society, needed to rescind invitations to five Jewish delegates after protests from extremist Islamic groups. Both the Houthi leadership and Mansur Hadi's government have turned a blind eye to targeted violence against religious minorities, with a particularly brazen attack occurring in March 2016 when gunmen killed 16 people at a home for the elderly in Aden run by the Catholic Missionaries of Charity. The growing popularity of Houthi and Salafi extremist ideology in Yemen does not bode well for the safety and security of Yemen's dwindling religious minorities.

9

EDUCATION AND SOCIETY

Beauty is all she knows.
O! Sana'a, wakening to the sparrow's chirrup,
    dozing off to the pigeon's coo,
        dreaming a flute floating tunes
            in a street near-by.
Her winter is timid and warm
    her summer is cool, gentle.
        In the springtime, households open
their windows in the early morning
to greet a gift of rose and lilac.
It's over.
She was drinking from a mountain spring
    when war startled her and the spring dried up.
She once had a stream—
    her gardens ache for it—
but the thundering decrees of a cannon
    forced it away.[1]
Abd al-Aziz al-Maqalih (1937–), "The 42nd Qasidah"

1. 'Abd Al-'Azīz Maqāliḥ, Bob Holman, and Sam Liebhaber. *The Book of Sana'a : Poetry of 'Abd Al-'Azīz Al-Maqāliḥ*. Yemen Translation Series (Ardmore, PA: American Institute for Yemeni Studies, 2004), 208–9.

What language is spoken in Yemen?

As nearly all foreign students discover after dedicating years to the study of the Arabic language, nobody actually speaks *fusha*, or formal Modern Standard Arabic. Each country in the Middle East and North Africa has its own version of colloquial (*'aamiyah*) Arabic based on a combination of other native languages, colonial history, and culture. There are local dialects (*lahjah*) that further differentiate residents of distinct regions within a single country. In mainland Yemen there are five main lahjah corresponding to the country's five geographic regions: Sana'a and the northern half of the country, Ta'iz and the middle region, Tihama and the western coastal areas, Aden and its immediate hinterland, and the eastern deserts and oases of Hadramawt. Within these regional lahjah there are also subdialects with subtle differences found in particular cities or among certain tribes. The linguistic outlier in Yemen is Soqotri, spoken primarily on the southern Yemeni island of Soqotra and its surrounding archipelago which is more closely related to Afro-Asiatic languages with roots in the oldest Semitic languages that ceased to exist thousands of years ago. The study of Soqotri, whose grammatical features no longer exist in Arabic, Hebrew, or Aramaic, helps scholars understand the prehistoric past and the gradual evolution of all Semitic languages. Once in danger of being lost to the more dominant national language of Arabic, Soqotri has recently experienced a resurgence as a new generation of Soqotrans has popularized Soqotri poetry and song as an expression of local cultural pride.

Reflective of local pride in the superiority of their country's history, culture, and language, many Yemenis claim that their local 'aamiya is the most authentic and the closest relative to the Classical Arabic of the Quran. This is certainly a subjective perception rather than a matter of phonological fact, further challenged by the apparent influence of African, Persian, and Asian languages on Yemeni Arabic's morphology. The authenticity of Yemen's lahjah notwithstanding, Sana'a has long been known as one of the best places to study Arabic, both for the ease of understanding the local dialect and for the total immersion experience, a consequence of the dearth of English speakers.

Beginning in the 19th century, there was a transition from oral to written religious instruction and legal decisions. Oral *shariah* instruction from teacher to student gave way to written dissemination through the gradual evolution of print and the influence of Ottoman and British educational styles on Yemeni society. While the written word insured longevity, the absence of the oral tradition obscured original meanings hidden within the tones of verbal recitation. Yemen's state school curriculum along with official correspondence and records are mostly in fusha Arabic.

The beauty of the Yemeni language is not in its written form but in the oral tradition that pervades every aspect of education, social life, and politics. The use of poetry in everyday life and the pride that tribes and leaders maintain in employing an official poet reflect the importance of the spoken word to Yemenis. No political gatherings, wedding ceremonies, funerals, or tribal arbitrations are complete without the sonorous voice of the local poet. Even a mundane bus ride may present passengers with a composition of comical prose lamenting the crowded public transportation options in Yemen. The centrality of poetry has gradually declined among new generations of Yemenis, especially those born and raised abroad to parents who migrated for employment, who show preference for the written word and social media. For those still being raised in traditional Yemeni societies and culture, there remains a strong emphasis on the rote memorization of influential poems and religious texts, even at the expense of written literacy.

What is the literacy rate in the general Yemeni population?

Illiteracy in Yemen remains a major obstacle to development, particularly among an older generation raised on the importance of oral education and memorization. The national literacy rate is around 50%, although only 30% for women, who experience disproportionate difficulty accessing education. Although these numbers reflect a 150% increase since 1994, owing to significant international investment in education, Yemen still ranks near the bottom of global literacy rates. At the same time, 88% of school-age boys and 77% of school-age girls attend primary school, a monumental increase when compared with the single-digit enrollments prior to 1970. Before the 2012 Arab Spring, there were only 16,000 schools for 135,000 villages and settlements. Among those were 4,500 religious schools whose curriculum and core subjects were not regulated by the Ministry of Education. Efforts to address deficiencies in the education system, train an additional 90,000 teachers, and increase girls' access to education were indefinitely put on hold by the current conflict, but will need to be addressed as a post-conflict priority.

The disparity between rising school enrollment and literacy rates can be attributed to the unfortunate fact that nearly 50% of Yemeni children drop out before secondary school, a statistic that is much higher for Yemeni girls living in rural regions where upward of 62% will not have graduated primary school. Government literacy centers, set up to address these alarming statistics, often lack funding, teaching materials, and qualified teachers. Particularly in rural areas, there are insufficient numbers of schools, often meaning that multiple villages will share the same small school, forcing students to travel long distances for subpar educational opportunities. While the lack of schooling can certainly be attributed to both the dearth of physical school buildings and the economic necessity of employing children to support the family, there is a cultural impediment as well. Girls are sometimes forced to remain at home rather than attend what are usually co-ed primary schools, in an effort to maintain a daughter's chastity and the honor of her family. In agricultural communities, families are also reliant on the participation of school-age girls in farm labor and cannot afford to send their daughters to school. The schools themselves are poorly equipped and do not have bathrooms or running water, thus adding to the multitude of challenges facing the education of women and girls in Yemen.

In many rural communities and in some urban settings, Yemeni women will marry early because of poverty and maintain a fertility rate near six children per mother, which in 2005 was one of the highest in the world. The lack of adequate skills and education has only served to perpetuate the cycle of women's dependence on male relatives or husbands. Women make up only 29% of the country's labor force, with the great majority confined to the house to care for large families and required to remain within the society-mandated respectable confines of the household.

Despite Western generalizations that early marriage, *shariah* Islamic law, and clothing restrictions are an insurmountable impediment to women's development in Yemen, programs promoting women's empowerment have been well received across the political and religious spectrum. Government agencies, Islamic groups, and civil society organizations support the establishment of microcredit, literacy, and education for women. Yemenis often take pride in their support of women, even if some of this support is subjective and limited to certain areas of politics and the economy.

Much of the initial investment in education during the 20th century was the product of the local development associations, or LDAs, which took advantage of the growing amount of remittances sent home by Yemenis working in Saudi Arabia, Kuwait, and other Gulf countries during the oil boom. These LDAs were set up to fund local community development projects such as schools, roads, health clinics, and agricultural development. Local initiatives started by the LDAs and other grassroots efforts were often supported by foreign donors whose grant funding was at times funneled through government bureaucracies, where corruption invariably reduced the total sums arriving to the communities.

Is there a tradition of higher education?

The most significant growth in the education sector since 1970 has been in higher education. The University of Sana'a, the largest and most-respected university in the country, was founded by Kuwait during the 1970s, along with a number of major hospitals. A similarly well-regarded university was opened in Aden by the PDRY. Other smaller academic centers and universities were opened in Hodeidah, Ibb, Ta'iz, Dhammar, and Hadramawt. By 2007, there were nearly 200,000 students enrolled, studying diverse subjects including science, education, business, agriculture, engineering, and Islamic law. Educated Yemenis, however, have few incentives to remain in the country because of limited employment prospects, meager funds for research or faculty salary, and a government that rewards nepotism rather than merit. A growing number of academics traveled abroad for doctoral or post-doctoral work and chose not to return, constituting a massive brain drain across the Yemeni university system. Standards have declined to the extent that recent BA graduates were called on to teach the very classes that they had recently attended. This has had a ripple effect throughout

Yemen's secondary and primary education as the universities have not been able to train a new generation of teachers.

University students were an important part of Arab Spring protests both in Yemen and around the Arab World. Since the onset of current hostilities in 2014, however, free expression in Yemeni universities has declined significantly as both faculty and students have been repeatedly arrested and threatened by the Houthi regime. The global Scholars at Risk program has continued to receive a growing number of applications from Yemeni scholars who were the target of Houthi intimidation and feared for their continued safety in Yemen.

Can women attend schools at any level?

In terms of women's access to education, there is a clear distinction between North and South Yemen. In the PDRY during the 1970s, there were equal numbers of girls and boys enrolled in primary and secondary schools and women actually outnumbered men in fields such as medicine and education. The port city of Aden, in particular, offered the best education and career advancement for Yemeni women, presenting a challenge to the religious-conservative cultural norms prevailing elsewhere in the country. In contrast to the education and employment opportunities offered to women in South Yemen, women in the North had far fewer options.

After unification in 1990, southern women saw their opportunities decline as women's education was opposed by the Islah Party and other religious conservatives, who enforced school gender segregation and targeted nascent women's study programs. Women have been recruited as largely figurehead candidates for national offices, even on the religiously conservative Islahi ticket, but these have been mainly limited to token "state feminist" positions with little actual influence other than placating international donors demanding increased equality.

In 1996, Dr. Raufah Hassan, one of Yemen's first female journalists and a leading academic feminist leader, founded the first Center for Women's Studies in Sana'a University with funding from the Dutch government. The Islah Party, Iman University, and Abdul Majeed al-Zindani immediately targeted what they perceived as the liberal and secular direction of the center and threatened Hassan's life, sending her into exile. Without Hassan's charismatic leadership the center was closed in 2000 at the behest of the Yemeni government under pressure from Islahis. Hassan sought temporary refuge in the Netherlands but returned to Yemen to lobby for women's rights and political participation before succumbing to cancer in 2011. Other Yemeni women, like Amat al-Alim Alsoswa, succeeded in obtaining an education either in Yemen or abroad, returning to Yemen to assume leadership positions in government and civil society.

What is the state of women's rights in Yemen?

In a region not known for women's rights, Yemen was the first and only state on the Arabian Peninsula to grant women's suffrage as part of increasing participation in the democratic experiment in the early 1990s. This was not particularly difficult as Yemen is also the only purely republican state on the peninsula and is surrounded by religious and socially conservative states with no democratic elections that are infamous for their absence of women's rights.

In South Yemen and specifically in Aden, under the socialist PDRY, women had significant rights and public roles, in contrast to the conservative religious policies enacted by the unified government after 1990. Despite a precipitous decline in the number of women in parliament from 1993 to 2003, the number of women voting has increased to match the number of men voting, thereby encouraging Yemeni politicians to consider women's issues in their campaigns. Nevertheless, in 2009, only 5% of women claimed membership in a political party, partly as a consequence of official Islah policy that claimed women to be "unfit for election." Even Amat al-Salam Raja, the first female member of the party's steering committee, said that "women's contributions are unfit given current political conditions." There is, nevertheless, a small faction within Islah that remains open to women's participation in the party.[2] The prohibition on gender mixing in public and private settings has further restricted opportunities for younger women to become politically involved or to serve as community leaders. There were positive signs among the younger generation of women who expressed

---

2. "Islah Deems Women Unfit for Election," *Yemen Today Magazine*, February 1, 2003.

interest in political and civic engagement during the Arab Spring protests in 2011. Two years later, the National Dialogue Conference (NDC) called for an ambitious political quota of 30% women, although it fell far short of its aim.

In the social realm, women are subject to domestic violence, sexual abuse by husbands, child marriage, and restricted freedom of movement, all of which are invariably underreported. These practices are far more prevalent in the country's coastal regions and the eastern Hadramawt where female genital mutilation occurs with greater frequency. In rural areas where health care falls far short of the minimum needed to treat what constitutes 70% of the country's population, women face the largest obstacle to accessing medical assistance. Women in some communities must be accompanied by a male relative or guardian and are economically dependent on a male member of the family, whether father or husband, thus often keeping even the closest medical facilities out of reach. There are relatively few female doctors and many Yemeni women would prefer to suffer and even die from gynecological issues rather than be subjected to examination by a male doctor. The absence of neonatal and obstetric care can lead to the subjugation of a second generation and the perpetual cycle of poverty, as babies born in the home are far less likely to be registered with the Yemeni government. Unregistered children cannot be forced into mandatory public primary education nor can accurate statistics be taken of precisely how many children are not in school. Recent changes in the country's healthcare system have allowed for the emergence of more women's health centers, although these developments have been stalled by the onset of hostilities in 2014.

The country's high birth rate is combined with an equally high infant and maternal mortality rate, ranking Yemen as one of the worst countries for women's reproductive health. The 2015 child mortality rate was 6%, a number that is remarkably lower than the 38% in 1950, but still among the highest in the world. Women are particularly disadvantaged in Yemen's healthcare system, evidenced by the fact that the leading causes of hospital morbidity are complications due to pregnancy, childbirth, and postpartum maternal care. Yemen's high birth rate is unlikely to decline in the near future as Yemen ranks among the lowest for the prevalence of modern contraceptive methods. Reduced rates of fertility would likely improve the economic health of Yemeni families and the overall quality and availability of healthcare for women. Low levels of education, legal and economic dependence on a husband, and increased threats of divorce in the context of abusive polygamous marriages leave very little opportunity for women to control their childbearing. In addition, Islamic religious doctrine does not condone contraception and Yemeni cultural traditions place an outsized inherent value on female fertility and specifically on a woman's ability to bear sons for her husband.

When do women usually marry and what rights do they have?

Hanging lightbulbs decorating the streets surrounding the groom's house and the *zaffah*, or procession are two of the telltale signs of wedding festivities. The wedding ceremony itself is often a festive and lavish occasion with food, dancing, religious and traditional customs, and qat chewing in gender-segregated venues. Expensive weddings and bridal dowries can be an impediment to young grooms who do not have the financial means to marry and support a wife according to the standards of local tradition. There is a significant underclass of Yemeni men who remain single for years until managing to save for a wedding. The current conflict has altered this pattern. Poverty and uncertainty have lowered the standards for celebrations and dowries, and families are finding it increasingly difficult to feed their children; therefore, they are more willing to part with their daughters for a bridal price that is less than customary.

Child brides in Yemen are not unusual. Poor families will often marry their young daughters to older men when they are no longer able to support them. Girls may even be betrothed before the age of 13, although generally the marriage is consummated only once the girl reaches puberty. Marriage contracts are overseen by a qadi, or religious judge, who ensures that the marriage is consensual. There are instances, however, where marriages are coerced, such as when a woman refuses a match arranged by her parents or if her actions may otherwise bring dishonor to the family. Polygamy is practiced openly in Yemen, and it is not uncommon to find wealthy men with four wives, some of whom may be his relatives.

There is no enforceable minimum age for marriage, nor is there any legal protection for a safe and responsible sex life within the context of marriage. The republic's penal code even specifies a wife's obligation to be sexually available to her husband at all times and deprives women of the ability to claim rape within a marriage. Furthermore, in some of the more conservative communities in Yemen, women do not have the right to request a divorce from their husbands without the intercession of a male guardian, although they may include certain conditions in their marriage contract, the violation of which would constitute grounds for divorce. Men, on the other hand, have the authority to divorce by oral declaration without required intercession or judicial approval.

The marriage of a daughter is usually preceded by two traditional payments. The *mahr*, or bridal payment, is given directly to the bride along with jewelry and clothing as an expression of love and devotion. The *shart*, is a payment to the bride's family as theoretical compensation for the loss of the daughter's future salary and economic contribution to the family unit. Inherited wealth from the woman's family, as well as wages earned in the workplace, do not automatically become the property of the husband under Islamic law.

Citizenship inheritance rights of Yemeni children differ for the mother and the father. The child of a Yemeni mother and a non-Yemeni father can only receive Yemeni citizenship if the foreign father dies, the couple is divorced, or the woman has been abandoned by the foreign husband. The child of a Yemeni man, on the other hand, receives immediate citizenship regardless of the mother's nationality. Property inheritance rights are similarly more restrictive for Yemeni mothers than they are for men. Although women are allowed by Yemeni law to enter the workforce, most are compelled by societal norms to remain in the household, thereby providing few opportunities for female entrepreneurship and public voice.

Are there any Yemeni women who have managed to succeed despite these obstacles?

Yemeni women such as Amat al-Alim Alsoswa, who occupied a senior leadership position in Saleh's General People's Congress political party and served as Yemen's ambassador to several European countries, represent the pre-revolutionary generation of women's liberation, when it was far more difficult to break society's cultural barriers to women's education and advancement. Alsoswa began her career as a journalist, becoming one of the country's most recognizable figures; she went on to serve as a leader in national women's movements and became a prominent global activist for gender equality in Yemen and across the Arab world. Other prominent Yemeni women, such as Raqia Hmeidan, one of the Arab world's foremost female scholars in the field of law, succeeded in obtaining an education abroad before returning to Yemen to become prominent in government and civil society.

This first generation of Yemeni women broke the glass ceiling for a new generation of Yemen's young women to continue their legacy both at home and abroad. For example, Tawakkul Karman, a member of the Islah Party, who was the first Arab woman to win the Nobel Peace Prize, founded the organization Women Journalists Without Chains. During the Arab Spring protests she became the voice of the *shabab*, or youth, directing criticism at both Saleh's government and at factions within the Islah Party. Not all the protesting youth felt comfortable with Karman as their spokesperson, with many criticizing her outsize cult of personality and her Islamist leanings, along with suspicious sources of financial support from Qatar and the Muslim Brotherhood. Both Tawakkul and her sister Safa, who was the first Yemeni to receive a degree from Harvard Law School, have become the public face of Yemeni youth abroad, often receiving prominent recognition from US and European governments and universities.

In the midst of a contentious and drawn-out battle in Ta'iz, several women have assumed leadership roles in the resistance movement and in the humanitarian struggle. Bushra al-Maqtari is a Yemeni writer and novelist from Ta'iz who was awarded the 2013 Françoise Giroud Award for Defence of Freedom and Liberties among other international awards. Her recent book *What You Left Behind? Voices from a Forgotten War-torn Country*, is a collection of firsthand accounts that she recorded during the current war. Professor Hayat al-Zahbani is a human rights activist who created a media initiative for women in Ta'iz. Her pioneering work in helping internationally displaced refugees was recognized in an award ceremony in 2017.

In addition to other unsung heroines of Ta'iz, dozens of Yemeni women have risen to prominence through their writing and public broadcasting. Nabil al-Zubair is Yemen's best-known female poet, an important mark of distinction in a country that has great respect for national poets and the art of oratory. Hadeel al-Yamani won the 2017 Courage in Journalism Award from the International Women's Media Foundation for her coverage of the war in Yemen and for her pioneering work as the first female television correspondent for Al Jazeera Arabic in Yemen.

Other Yemeni women have succeeded as artists and actresses, such as Saly Hamada, a popular actress who is leading a revolution in the entertainment industry to allow a greater public role for women. These women continue to challenge the cultural, patriarchal, and religious constraints and taboos in Yemeni society and carry with them hope for a far better future for the women of their country.

What is the role of civil society in modern Yemen?

The term "civil society" was popularized during the 1980s to describe the non-state grassroots actors working to undermine authoritarian regimes in Eastern Europe and Latin America. Civil society came to include NGOs, community groups, labor unions, charities, religious organizations, and professional associations. Stereotypes of tribal and Islamic societies have perpetuated assumptions about the dearth of local activism in an inherently conservative Middle Eastern society. Few would expect to find a robust civil society in Yemen, a country known for its weak central government and dispersed political power.

The modern states of North and South Yemen were both founded by grassroots organizations that toppled the ruling regimes. In the North, the Free Yemen Movement and groups of local dissidents founded an anti-imamate coalition that overthrew the religious institution in 1962. In the South, Aden was home to the Arab world's first and only "proletarian" revolution, led by labor unions formed during the 1950s. The Aden Trade Union Congress (ATUC), formed during the 1950s, grew into a militant labor movement, paralyzing the Aden economy through strikes and mass protests and contributing to the nationalist revolution that toppled the British colony of Aden.

There is a long history of civil society in Yemen in several areas of the economy, religion, and education. Majlis al-tijara, or council of merchants, was an important component of 19th- and 20th-century Sana'a and Tarim, as the local groups determined prices and taxes and collectively paid for night watchmen. The absence of government institutions and the preference for local autonomy led to the proliferation of local development associations (LDA) in Yemen during the 1970s. Local and regional LDAs consolidated funds made available by foreign donors and worker remittances to build roads, schools, irrigation systems, and other communal projects. The country's education was similarly organized around Zaydi and Salafi religious organizations that funded school construction and trained a generation of teachers to supplement, and often replace, the inadequate government schooling system.

Yemen's vibrant civil society has acted to fill the gap left for decades by poor government administration. While supporting vital communal needs through their activities, LDAs and networks of religious schools have managed to divert government resources to their own local causes and doctrinal agendas. Without central oversight, LDAs do not always coordinate construction efforts, leading to redundancy and the absence of a logical nationwide network of roads and infrastructure. Additionally, the country's national curriculum is reaching fewer students, resulting in a system of education that further fragments societies rather than working to promote a single Yemeni identity. Notwithstanding, given the levels of corruption, nepotism, and mismanagement in Yemen's state government, it is unlikely that central planning would produce better results than LDAs and local religious organizations.

Another form of civil society and free expression is the country's media. Following the 1994 Civil War, Yemen's media expanded to include two competing broadcast companies, two national daily newspapers, a proliferation of satellite dishes, and a significant increase in the number of periodicals. Newspaper readership has reached even illiterate segments of the population, who regularly gather for group news readings. Print media, however, was tightly controlled by Yemeni political parties such as the General People's Congress, the Yemen Socialist Party, and the Islah Party who owned most of the large-scale printing presses in the country. This made the proliferation of internet news and social media all the more transformative as its power to mobilize popular support outside the realm of state dominance essentially seized control of local media from the government.

The Arab Spring revolution brought about a massive expansion of Yemen's civil society to include 8,300 registered organizations by June 2014. This civil society renaissance came to an abrupt halt with the onset of hostilities in late 2014 and increasing concern about a growing humanitarian crisis. With several exceptions, most civil society activity has come to revolve around humanitarian aid, foreign disaster relief, and merely surviving the crisis as a community.

What is the state of healthcare in Yemen?

Prior to unification in 1990, there was a stark difference between the quality and availability of healthcare available in North and South Yemen. In the South, the PDRY inherited a British healthcare model based on the UK's National Health Service that offered free care to all its citizens. In the socialist society of the PDRY, healthcare was treated as a basic right and was entirely controlled by the state. The Mutawakkilite Kingdom of Yemen (1918–1962) had little or no healthcare aside from modest facilities in Sana'a, Ta'iz, and Hodeidah. During the 1960s, Egyptian occupation forces first established a government healthcare system in the country's urban centers; this was supplemented in remote northern areas by the International Red Cross, which opened several mobile clinics. Unlike the PDRY, the YAR made allowances for private clinics and hospitals, many of which were funded by neighboring Arab oil states, while others were run by US- and European-based philanthropies and religious organizations. For example, in 1964, the Southern Baptist Mission from the United States was given permission to open a hospital in Jibla, a village near Ta'iz. This hospital and its medical missionaries brought Western medicine to this remote rural region for nearly four decades until an al-Qaeda affiliate murdered the missionaries in an attack on the hospital in December 2002.

The Public Health Services now available in the united Republic of Yemen are a combination of state-funded institutions in the South and private facilities in the North. Hospitals and clinics remain concentrated in urban areas, which combined with rising fees have made healthcare inaccessible, especially to Yemen's poorest rural population. Prior to the current conflict, many of these areas were serviced only by NGOs like Doctors without Borders and the International Committee of the Red Cross (ICRC), who set up clinics offering free healthcare to locals. While well intentioned, these internationally funded medical facilities have fostered a growing dependency on foreign aid in the field of medicine. Many of these programs have focused on specific diseases or health initiatives, drawing medical professionals away from primary care and toward the better pay offered by programs orchestrated by foreign donors. The inadequacy of emergency and ambulatory services, in particular, was brought to international attention when Aden was chosen to host the "Khaleeji 20" football tournament, or the Arabian Gulf Cup, in December 2010, exposing the city's and the country's inadequate health facilities to a global viewership.

Yemen's total annual expenditure on healthcare prior to the conflict was around 5% of GDP. Less than half of this cost was paid by the government; the balance of medical bills was paid from private "out of pocket" spending and some foreign aid. In fact, 95% of Yemenis resort to the private sector for at least a portion of their health needs. Despite high dependence on private expenditure, the overwhelming majority of Yemenis do not have health insurance.

Poor sanitation and contaminated water sources lead to health crises that continue to overwhelm the country's inadequate medical facilities. Large segments of the population continue to contract cholera and other water-borne diseases along with schistosomiasis (bilharzia) and other worm infestations from a lack of government sewage treatment and irregular garbage pickup from crowded urban streets and beaches. Warm temperatures combine with trash overflow and periodic flooding during the monsoon season to spread debilitating mosquito-borne diseases like malaria and dengue fever.

Disparities between rich and poor Yemenis are particularly pronounced in healthcare, as Yemenis who can afford it will travel abroad for treatment in Jordan, India, and European countries where visas can be obtained for wealthier Yemenis. Meanwhile, the 16 million Yemenis who live outside the main city centers of Aden, Hodeidah, Mukalla, Sana'a, and Ta'iz can scarcely afford the costs of transportation, accommodation, medical and drug fees, and lost earnings for a visit to urban healthcare facilities. The prohibitively expensive medical care, which is inaccessible to nearly 50%

of the population, is made even more inaccessible by the dearth of Yemeni doctors. The country has one of the worst ratios of medical professionals to patients in the world. Yemen's healthcare system is reliant on doctors, nurses, and other medical professionals from countries like China and Russia, but these are often forced to leave the country during times of conflict or restricted travel due to airport closings. The dire condition of Yemen's healthcare before the onset of hostilities in 2014 helps to explain how and why the most recent conflict has impacted the population so drastically.

10

THE ARAB SPRING IN YEMEN

The soul of this city floats
above the flood of Time.
  Do not wake her
  Let her sigh while her children cough.
  Do not kindle a light in her vacant alleys.
There is still blood in those alleys—too much, too sweet—
the blood of a martyr who lived justice
  but turned the page of life too soon.
Let Sana'a sleep and forget.
Let Sana'a sleep and remember.
Never desecrate a tomb with thundering speeches,
  a tomb settled by grief.
On its roof are outcast mourners
  and underneath, lost corpses.[1]
          —Abdulaziz Al-Maqaleh (1937–), "The 47th Qasidah"

How did the Arab Spring manifest in Yemen?

The Arab Spring arrived in Yemen as a wave of popular dissent directed against the regime of Ali Abdullah Saleh in early 2011. This was not the first time that Yemenis had protested against Saleh during his 33 years as president. What made this round of public

---

1. 'Abd Al-'Azīz Maqāliḥ, Bob Holman, and Sam Liebhaber. *The Book of Sana'a : Poetry of 'Abd Al-'Azīz Al-Maqāliḥ*. Yemen Translation Series (Ardmore, PA: American Institute for Yemeni Studies, 2004), 232–33.

demonstrations unique was both the scale of the participants in terms of sheer numbers and their ability to cut across political, religious, and gender boundaries in their opposition to the president. Although the movement was termed the "youth" revolution, participants were of all ages, united in their economic, societal, and political marginalization and disenfranchisement. Debating the future of Yemen was no longer limited to conversations held among the intellectual and military elite but was now conducted openly through social media, made available to any Yemeni with an internet connection.

The new generation of Yemeni youth, in particular, was given the space and tools to participate in politics outside the purview of their elders. The very location of the protests in Change Square (Sahat al-Taghiyir), in front of the new Sana'a University campus, reflected the movement's youth and educational aspirations. No group benefited more from this revolution than Yemen's women, who experienced a social renaissance during the protests. Previously limited to prescribed household tasks and segregated areas of society, women now had the space—both physical and digital—to contribute by organizing demonstrations, disseminating news, giving lectures, raising money, appearing in public at the site of the protests, and addressing the global media.

Prior to 2011, the taboos on mixed-gender socializing in Yemen were just beginning to face small-scale challenges from a thriving café and restaurant culture that catered to Yemen's youth. The expansion of primary and secondary schooling led to delayed marriages and the mixing of sexes in education and in the workplace, outside the social limitations of the family home. At Change Square, a woman was able to join the protests, frequent what had previously been men-only restaurants, and even stay overnight in the protest camp without subjecting herself or her family to accusations of 'ayb, or shamefulness. Saleh used this issue as a way to stoke division and dissent within the ranks of protest supporters in his infamous April 2011 speech in which he implied that the women of Change Square were all "loose" women, a designation seen as a great insult to female activists and a dishonor to their families and tribes. Thousands of women took to the streets in protest of Saleh's degradation of women, while at the same time the fathers, brothers, and husbands of those women in Change Square were forced to deal with the conservative religious backlash emanating from Saleh's inflammatory speech. This freedom was short-lived, as groups of Salafis ultimately seized control of the protests after the initial weeks and established strict gender segregation and, in the process, coopted the revolution from Yemen's youth and women.

The public protests and accompanying online media attention led to the proliferation of young Yemeni musicians who symbolized the popular movement. Ahmed Asery and his band 3 Meters Away used reggae, rock, and blues fusion in their popular revolutionary songs: "Inhale Freedom" and "I'm Staying Till the Regime Leaves." Urban artists like Murad Subai' painted slogans and images on the walls of Sana'a and led the famous "The Walls Remember" campaign, which memorialized the victims of Saleh's regime. Young Yemeni comedians have also used the streets and online forums to introduce humor to the tragic events and the absurdity of some political groups and individuals. Muhammad al-Ruba, for example, has risen to internet fame for his political satire of the Houthi leadership and the remnants of Yemen's republican government. The freedom and opportunity presented to young artists were a clear departure from earlier government censorship. For instance, Fahd al-Qarni, a popular comedian and singer, had been arrested in 2009 and sentenced to 18 months in jail for insulting President Saleh and encouraging southern separatists.

Who else joined the youth protesters?

Yemen's youth were joined by two existing popular movements from the North and the South with a long history of conflict with Saleh. The Houthis, also known as Ansar Allah, were the most surprising attendees at Yemen's Arab Spring protests. That is not because they had the fewest grievances against Saleh, who was considered their principal enemy and responsible for the loss of countless lives and property. Rather, after six inconclusive wars with the Sana'a government between 2004 and 2010, the Houthis saw these protests as a way to bring their movement to the capital and transform their war against Saleh from a conflict in the country's northern periphery to a cause célèbre at its center.

The Houthis were joined by members of al-Hirak al-Janubi, or the Southern Movement. Similar to their counterparts in the North, al-Hirak had already been in the midst of its own protest movement against Saleh based in Aden and other southern areas. Since their defeat in the 1994 civil war, southerners had grown irate over the blatant theft of natural resources, land, and political power by Saleh's regime. The president was accused of lining his personal pockets with profits from oil fields located in the former PDRY, without reinvesting any of the money in South Yemen. Popular protests, which gradually increased after 2007, were met with violence by Saleh's forces, leading many southerners to call for an independent South Yemen and the reemergence of the PDRY flag as a symbol of their resistance to northern occupation.

The last group to officially join the protests was Hizb al-Islah, Saleh's main political opposition, which had become part of the Joint Meeting Parties (JMP) in 2005, although individual party members had been present in Change Square far earlier. The JMP had previously called for political reforms within the democratic process rather than for Saleh's resignation, a stance that was changed in March 2011 as Salafi students from Abdul-Majid al-Zindani's al-Iman University joined the youth movement in Sana'a. The appearance of religious students allied with Islah alongside their Zaydi religious opposition and the country's secular youth was one of the most captivating moments and images of the protests. Tribal elements also joined the anti-Saleh protests after Sadiq and Hamid al-Ahmar, the two most prominent leaders of the Hashid tribal confederation, announced their support for the demonstrations. Change Square had indeed become a political rainbow for nearly every element of Yemeni society.

The protests began with a call for true democratic reform and for Saleh's resignation. Following the model used by the Arab Spring protests in Tunisia and Egypt, Yemen's youth gathered thousands through social media. After anti-protest violence on March 18, 2011, however, the movement was coopted by seasoned political elites who saw these popular protests as a way to solidify their own political gains. The protestors were no longer a youth movement against a repressive dictator, but a microcosm of Yemen's political groups transposed to the streets of Sana'a and other major urban areas. Having lost some of their initial revolutionary fervor and optimism, Al-Hirak leaders chose to withdraw from the protests and were keen to disassociate themselves from the "revolution" rather than becoming mired in North Yemen politics. Other groups like Islah and the Houthis remained, to entrench themselves in a popular revolution that would drag the country into its most recent civil war.

What were the main highlights of the protests in Yemen?

Anti-Saleh protests gained the most traction and popular sympathy following the tragic events of March 18, 2011, a day that became known as the "Friday of Dignity." As protesters rose from their Friday prayers, snipers loyal to Saleh's regime fired into the crowd killing 50 worshippers. The public uproar following the killings galvanized the JMP along with many tribal leaders and senior officers of the military to part ways with Saleh and join the protesters. Foremost among the defections from Saleh's camp was General Ali Muhsin al-Ahmar, the president's childhood friend, on whom he had relied for military campaigns against southern secessionists and northern Houthi rebels. Al-Ahmar's declaration of support for the protests was considered a true victory for the revolution, while at the same time it was a demonstration of how quickly politics in Yemen can change to meet new circumstances. Al-Ahmar, previously one of the most notorious military commanders, who was responsible for death and suffering in the northern and southern regions of the country, was now aligned with his former victims in protest against Saleh, a president with whom he seemed to have had an inseparable political and personal allegiance. His support was not received positively by many activists who were suspicious of his motives, thought to be related to succession politics, and they distrusted him after years of his being involved in the corruption of the Saleh regime.

Urban protests were soon accompanied by rising violence and bombings across the country. Saleh's Republic Guards began clashing with Ali Muhsin's army and Hashid tribal militias led by the sons of Sheikh Abdullah al-Ahmar, the head of the Hashid Federation. In response, Ali Muhsin placed his troops as a cordon around Change Square both to protect the protestors and to portray himself as their champion. The violence reached a crescendo on June 3, 2011, when Saleh's palace mosque was bombed, severely injuring the president and sending him to Saudi Arabia for medical treatment. Of equal consequence was the death of Abd al-Aziz 'Abd al-Ghani, one of the original founders of the 1962 Yemeni republic, who was praying next to Saleh during the attack. When 'Abd al-Ghani's death was announced on August 22, there was a public outpouring of grief for the loss of a republican hero, whose death symbolized Saleh's downfall and the disintegration of the republic built on the backs of Yemen's original revolutionary generation. It also marked one of the few moments of concordance when both the protesters and members of Saleh's regime came together for a day of mourning, not only for 'Abd al-Ghani, but for an era of Yemen's history that was unraveling. Saleh's hiatus was brief as he returned to Sana'a on September 23, 2011, much to the chagrin of his opponents, who assumed he had used his medical condition as a ruse for escaping prosecution.

How were the protests finally dissolved and what kind of compromise was reached?

On November 23, 2011, Saleh signed the Gulf Cooperation Council (GCC) Initiative, abdicating his position to his vice president and beginning a two-year transitional process that would culminate in a new constitution and free elections. According to the agreement, Saleh and his family were granted immunity from prosecution and he was allowed to retain his position as head of the General People's Congress (GPC). His embezzled funds were rumored to remain in foreign bank accounts. Over the subsequent three months, the JMP, which was made up of seven parties including Islah, was granted half the positions in the new government while the other half was retained for the GPC with Saleh at its head, a division that came to constitute a serious obstacle to governance. Islah's political success was ushered in by strategic tribal connections, with the al-Ahmar family in particular, along with a network of well-funded NGOs like the al-Islah Charitable Society and educational institutes such as the University of Science and Technology headed by tribal leader Tariq Abu Luhum. The Islah Party's success and longevity had been in its ability to avoid political controversy by remaining in the background of major decisions and waiting for the right moment to enter an advantageous position. This was true of Islah's policies during the post–Arab Spring protests' National Dialogue Conference (NDC), where the party's leaders refrained from insisting on Islamic shariah law and even accepted the concept of a federalist state despite their platform calling for a unitary Yemeni state with a strong central government. Islah's persistence and strategic navigation was awarded with outsized political representation in the transition government.

Muhammad Ba Sindwa, a native Adeni with a long political career, was given the post of prime minister in order to placate southerners, while Saleh's former vice president, Abd Rabbuh Mansur Hadi, was elected president to oversee the two-year transition period. The fact that Hadi ran unopposed in Yemen's first post-revolutionary elections only served to deepen public skepticism by those who argued that the revolution had failed to change Yemeni politics. Saleh was still a central figure in the country's politics and the new transitional government was bereft of representation from Yemen's youth movement, al-Hirak, or the Houthis, three groups who played central roles in early Arab Spring protests. The latter two groups charted a different path in an effort to claim political victories following the revolution.

While more moderate factions of the Houthi movement participated in the overthrow of Saleh in Sana'a, a more militant wing remained in northern Yemen. Under the leadership of Abdullah al-Hakim, the successful Houthi general of growing mythical proportions, the armed conquest of Sa'dah continued unabated. By the end of March 2011, the Houthis had already managed to install Fares Mana'a, one of Yemen's most notorious arms dealers and an opportunistic Houthi supporter, as governor of Sa'dah, replacing the pro-Saleh Taha Hajer who fled the region by helicopter.

Despite not being given a political voice in the transitional government, the Houthi movement was presented with a golden opportunity to consolidate its political base around the Sa'dah governorate without interference from the fractured government and military. By the end of 2011, trips up to the Sa'dah region already required a switch from government to Houthi checkpoints. Houthi tribesmen laid siege to and conquered Dammaj, the spiritual capital of the Salafi movement in northern Yemen, before spreading their military dominion to the surrounding governorates of Hajja, 'Amran, and al-Jawf. Salafi schools and loyalists were specifically targeted as part of the Zaydi revivalist campaign espoused by the Houthi movement. Al-Hakim's military conquest reached a crescendo in January 2014 with the campaign in 'Amran that seized the ancestral tribal territories of the powerful and influential al-Ahmar brothers. The divided and powerless Sana'a government was preoccupied in overseeing a successful transition and consolidating political power in the capital city rather than addressing Houthi territorial expansion in the rural and tribal areas of northern Yemen.

In the South, al-Hirak returned from Sana'a with a renewed determination to establish an independent South Yemen, divorced from the open political nepotism of the GCC Initiative. Al-Hirak members were, and continue to be, divided between those advocating complete independence from North Yemen and those preferring a greater degree of autonomy within a united Yemeni federalist system. The grassroots Southern Movement staged civil protests, lectures, and other non-violent demonstrations against the transitional government. A new generation of southerners, many of whom were not alive during the bloody 1986 civil war, could only recall the PDRY as a socialist utopia rather than an impoverished and politically violent state, home to global terrorist networks. Indeed, with generous financial support from the Soviet Union and China, South Yemen had achieved full employment, food and economic security, free medical services, a widespread expansion of education, and progressive social policies that benefited women in particular. Nationalist pride and short-term memories tend to skip over the oppressive elements of the socialist regime, the absence of political discourse, and multiple episodes of widespread violence.

As both the Houthis and al-Hirak sought to take advantage of the political void as a result of the GCC Initiative, it was al-Qaeda of the Arabian Peninsula (AQAP) that stood to gain the most from the uncertainty. The absence of a centralized and united Yemeni military and police force during the transition period allowed AQAP affiliates to overrun entire towns in the southern Yemeni province of Abyan in 2011, an unfortunate turn of events that many Yemenis blamed on Saleh's longtime support of al-Qaeda elements in Yemen for his own political gain. In the absence of government oversight, AQAP was able to provide a semblance of order for the local population, even managing to restore public utilities and security. Less than a year later, local residents of Abyan were caught in a crossfire between AQAP and "Popular Committees" made up of local fighters, segments of the Yemeni army, and US military support. With few rules of engagement, scores of civilians were killed, public buildings were leveled, and thousands were forced to flee to Aden as displaced persons.

The end of Saleh's presidency presented the country with a promising era of opportunity, leading to the formation of new political parties and overall optimism for political change. Among this collection of parties was a previously apolitical group of quietist Salafis who were traditionally skeptical of Yemeni politics. In March 2012 they formed the Rashad Union, headed by 'Abd al-Wahhab al-Humayqani and supported by two major Salafi charitable organizations: the Yemeni Wisdom Charity Association and the Benevolent Association. The Rashad Union was far more interested in spreading Salafi doctrine than in participating in a democracy, but they were willing to forgo their differences in political philosophy for a new publicity venue.

Several members of Saleh's GPC broke off and formed their own transitional parties, including the Bhakil Federation sheikh Muhammad Abu Luhum's Justice and Construction Party, which he modeled after the Turkish Justice and Development Party, hoping to appeal to both the Houthis and al-Hirak on federalist lines. Even while violence spread in the North and South and popular protests continued in Aden, the transitional government insisted on supporting the deliberations of the National Dialogue Conference (NDC). It was as if Sana'a and its political elite existed as its own state, divorced from the proceedings in surrounding governorates.

What kind of transitional government emerged?

The highlight of Yemen's post–Arab Spring transitional government was the National Dialogue Conference (NDC), which lasted from March 18, 2013, to January 25, 2014. Tribal sheikhs and other local representatives arrived en masse for what was termed a "historic moment" by Jamal Benomar, UN special envoy to Yemen. While 565 delegates, representing large segments of the population, conducted contentious debates about federalism and issued declarations affirming the positive direction of the Yemeni state, the only thing historic about the NDC was the hotel bill. The Movenpick Hotel, one of Yemen's only five-star establishments, was a major destination for the country's political elite. As long as the bills were paid, the conference continued to churn out statements exuding hope for reconciliation and state building. When the NDC adjourned, however, the delegates needed to leave their luxury hotel rooms and return to the reality of their constituents, who did not unanimously support the NDC outcomes.

In a conference dominated by skepticism and ill-fated efforts to placate the expectations of international observers financing the government's transition, there were several positive highlights. At the insistence of Jamal Benomar, the NDC needed to represent the voices of protest, mainly youth movements, women, minorities, and southerners. Representation was granted to each of these groups. There was even talk of including a representative from Yemen's small remaining Jewish community, but this plan was withdrawn after vocal Islamist opposition. Women made up 28% of the delegates and were drafted in large numbers into the ranks of the country's political establishment. This was indeed a recognition of the central and visible role that women had played in the early days of the revolution. While women had been promised a 30% quota of elected and appointed government positions, Yemeni politics are inherently patriarchal, leaving little room for a new generation of female politicians. Tawakkul Karman, the Nobel laureate and symbolic voice of the revolution, even went so far as to boycott the NDC, which she argued had retained the elite leadership of the previous regime to the exclusion of youth and women. This was part of what Yemenis referred to as the "hijacked revolution," an accusation often leveled at al-Ahmar and the political elite who joined the protests under the guise of "protecting" the revolution. This patriarchal hijacking extended well beyond the NDC as Rana Ghanem, assistant secretary of the Yemeni Popular Nasserist Party, was the only female representative at the December 2018 peace talks in Stockholm, a clear demonstration of the short-lived Yemeni commitments to increased women's political participation.

Although there were representatives from both the Houthis and from South Yemen at the NDC, but the seeds of the current civil war had already been sown. While the Houthis continued their territorial expansion in the North, their party's delegates were actively participating in the NDC, influencing its final outcome both from Sana'a and Sa'dah. Al-Hirak, which had abandoned Sana'a many months earlier, did not return to the capital city for the NDC and refused to accept its conclusions. Those southern representatives who did show up at the NDC were presented with the unenviable position of returning home having compromised southern autonomy and dismissed the economic and political grievances that had originally sparked their 2007 opposition movement. The disappointing conclusion of the NDC therefore only served to solidify the position and popularity of southern hardliners.

The United Nations finally pressured the transitional government to bring the NDC to a conclusion on January 21, 2014, more than six months after it was scheduled to conclude according to the original GCC Initiative timeframe. Nine individual working groups produced 1,800 recommendations, which were to be part of a new Yemeni constitution. It was far easier to issue uncontroversial statements than it was to arrive at a decisive conclusion regarding the fundamental issues that faced the Yemeni republic, specifically the structure and shape of the new government, the political centrality of Sana'a, and the equitable division of natural resources.

The most contentious issue emanating from the NDC constitutional discussions was the issue of federalism. President Mansur Hadi released plans for a six-region federal system that would partition the northern tribal areas into three. The Houthis had coveted the western coastal areas of the Tihama, and the port city of Hodeidah in particular. The six-region division, however, left the Houthis landlocked and without access to the eastern petroleum and water resources in the Saba desert region of Jawf and Marib provinces. Jamal Benomar, UN special envoy to Yemen, and secretary general of the NDC Ahmed Bin Mubarak held a meeting with Abdulmalek al-Houthi shortly after the six-region announcement, trying to persuade the Houthis to entertain the idea of a federalist system, to which Abdulmalek reportedly responded that there were only two Yemens—North and South. This thinly veiled attempt to divide and weaken the Houthi movement was formalized in a draft constitution released in January 2015, further fueling political tensions between President Hadi and the Houthi militias who already occupied the capital city.

How did the transitional government portray the conflict in Yemen's northern highlands?

As part of the NDC, a subcommittee on Sa'dah was formed to address controversial issues such as the disarmament of all parties in the conflict and renewed efforts to integrate the northern regions into a central state based in Sana'a. The subcommittee's final report addressed the underlying causes of Saleh's conflict with the Houthis. These included local grievances against the government for contributing to a lack of developmental investment, foreign interference that disrupted the historical coexistence of Zaydi and Sunni Muslims in the northern regions, and Saleh's divide-and-rule politics that fractured northern unity.

What emerged from both the Sa'dah subcommittee and from the NDC more generally was a redefinition of Yemen as a "participatory state," providing equal political representation without marginalizing any particular group. The Houthis championed this concept and added additional stipulations that called for the release of prisoners from the Sa'dah wars (2004–2010), compensation for victims of the wars, and the establishment of a commission of inquiry into the conduct of the wars. For good measure the Houthis added to the resolution a commitment by the Yemeni government to forgo secret agreements with the United States that allowed for drone operations over Yemeni territory, criminalizing the use of the national military in internal conflicts, and a guarantee that northern representatives would have equal representation in government agencies and in the armed forces.

Hadi's post-NDC announcement declaring his intention to form a federal state of six regions seemed to conflict with the ambiguous commitments made earlier to Houthi and southern representatives. The resolutions issued by the Sa'dah subcommittee were not implemented and fell from public consciousness, which had already shifted attention to the expansion in the southern regions of Ansar al-Shari'a, an al-Qaeda affiliate. In response, the Houthi military commander Abdullah al-Hakim seized the areas of territory in 'Amran and Hajja that had been intentionally separated from the North by the six-region federalist proposal. 'Amran's symbolism was twofold both as the hometown of Islah's Abdullah bin Husayn al-Ahmar and as the seat of the Hashid Tribal Confederation.

What truly alarmed Houthi representatives was the extent to which Islah and other Salafis had staked out an influential position in the new Yemeni government. After entering Sana'a in September 2014, the Houthis first targeted Ali Muhsin and his armored brigade, who were responsible for a great deal of carnage during the Houthis

Wars. The next target of the Houthi tribesmen were those institutions and leaders most closely associated with Islah. The Salafi al-Iman University was closed, eliminating 'Abd al-Majid al-Zindani's pulpit and a main source of radical recruits. Both Ali Muhsin and al-Zindani were reported to have fled the country shortly after the Houthi arrival in Sana'a, while Muhammad Qahtan, another prominent leader of the Islah Party, was taken captive and remains unaccounted for. Muhammad Qahtan's home and those of other Islahi affiliates like Tawakkul Karman were looted; many fled the country while others were arrested or compelled to adopt a low profile and not interfere with Houthi governance. Houthi targeting of Salafi organizations, both in the northern regions and in Sana'a, led to the rumor that Hadi had invited the Houthis to Sana'a to rid his transitional government of the Islahi opposition, only to realize belatedly that the northern tribesmen would not be satisfied until their fundamental grievances were addressed by the new Yemeni government.

When and why did the transition government fail?

When the Houthis entered Sana'a en masse in September 2014, only the most optimistic analysts believed that Hadi's government could emerge unscathed. However, if there was one moment that marked the failure of the transitional government, it was on January 22, 2015, when President Mansur Hadi and Prime Minister Khaled Bahah both submitted their resignations and were subsequently placed under house arrest in Sana'a and later fled to Aden. How did Hadi dig a political hole so deep that the only way out was resignation and an escape to Aden? His first mistake was pushing through a transitional process despite the fact that the most powerful political stakeholders had not yet agreed on critical questions about the identity of the post-Saleh Yemeni state. The six-region federal structure was rejected by the Houthis, who were aghast at Hadi's audacity in planning to truncate the regions of Hajja, al-Jawf, and 'Amran all while Houthi tribesmen completed the conquest of these very same northern territories. Dividing the South into two regions was seen as an attack on southern autonomy, especially as al-Hirak had boycotted the NDC. Despite the opposition, Hadi announced the formation of an NDC-recommended Constitution Drafting

Committee on March 8, 2014, as a political gambit to create new political entities as obstacles to the republic's two greatest threats.

Under the banner of continuing the 2011 revolution, the Houthis advanced on the capital city of Sana'a in September 2014 and pressured Hadi to consider the Peace and National Partnership Agreement, endorsed by Special Envoy Jamal Benomar and by most of the other Yemeni political parties. The new agreement would have increased Houthi political power at the expense of the old tribal elites and GPC and Islah stalwarts who dominated the transitional government. The new consensual government would be tasked with fighting corruption, overseeing economic development, and reintroducing the fuel subsidies recently cut by Hadi's government. In return, the Houthis would go back to Sa'dah. On January 17, 2015, when Hadi refused to rescind plans for a six-region federal state, Houthi gunmen kidnapped his then chief of staff, Ahmed bin Mubarak, seeking to use him as bargaining leverage. Over the next week, the city erupted in violence as the Houthis occupied the presidential palace with the assistance of armed forces still loyal to Saleh, prompting the resignation of Hadi and Bahah. Bin Mubarak was released after two weeks under condition that he leave Yemen permanently, which he promptly did and later took on the position of Yemeni ambassador to the United States.

By January 30, 2015, Hadi and his entire cabinet had been placed under house arrest, leaving the Houthis free to organize a separate National Conference. On February 6, the Houthis announced the formation of their own transitional national council consisting of 551 members and a five-person presidential council. Neither political body would have any real political power as a Supreme Revolutionary Council was formed in parallel, giving Abdulmalek's cousin Muhammad al-Houthi administrative power. The political maneuvering came to a halt when Hadi and his family escaped house arrest and fled to the southern port city of Aden toward the end of February 2015, marking the official end of the transitional government and the beginning of yet another costly civil war.

11

YEMEN'S MODERN CIVIL WAR

We left prison sniffing the air
  like a lion leaving its thicket
We walk on the edges of blades
  and approach the very gates of death
We refuse to live a life defiled
  by the oppression of a tyrant and his minions
We'll heap scorn on the machinations of the mighty
  when they send their minions to block our way.
We known that judgment is upon us
  and that circumstances have their reasons.
Our nation will come to learn that we
  have committed to the struggle for love of her
If we should be victorious . . . how often
  does hardship melt away from the zealous!
If we should meet our end, then how beautiful it is
  when Fate finds its suitor![1]

—Muhammad al-Zubayri (1910–1965), "On Leaving
Yemen . . . A Giant Prison"

What were the short-term causes of the current conflict in Yemen?

The Sa'dah wars (2004–2010) between Saleh's government and
the Houthis ended without addressing the root causes of northern

1. Muḥammad Maḥmūd al-Zubayrī, *Ṣalāḥ fī al-jaḥīm*. Sana'a: Dār al-Kalima, 1985.
   Translated by Sam Liebhaber, 55–58.

grievances against the Yemeni government. To their ultimate advantage, the Houthis were left with strategic military positions in the al-Jawf and Ma'rib regions. Between March 2011 and September 2014, while the rest of the country was overthrowing Saleh and setting up a transitional government, the Houthis were expanding their territorial possessions through military conquest, political alliances, popularization of their Zaydi revivalist movement, and their infamous slogan that appealed to Yemenis across religious or political spectrums: "Death to America! Death to Israel! Curse upon the Jews and Victory for Islam!"

Those targeted by the expansion of the Houthi movement included Salafi religious extremists and tribal opposition groups who had supported the Yemeni government's war against the north since 2004. An important turning point occurred in January 2014, when Houthi tribesmen destroyed the ancestral home compound of the al-Ahmar family near Khamir, symbolically toppling the power and prestige of the strongest tribal confederation in Yemen. The family's patriarch and leader of the Hashid confederation, Sheikh Abdullah bin Husayn bin Nasser al-Ahmar, had been one of the country's most powerful and influential figures until his death in 2007. The humiliation experienced by the al-Ahmar family and the overt demonstration of the weakened state of the Hashid confederation was likened by the Yemeni press to the "fall of the Pharaohs," as it completely upended the balance of power in northern Yemen.

Quite a few observers were surprised by the military prowess and adept political organization of the Houthi movement, which just a few years earlier had been reeling from six costly and destructive wars with the Yemeni government. The specific targeting of Salafis, supporters of the Islah opposition party, and of the Hashid tribal hierarchy were ambitious and well-planned operations aimed at not only recovering lost power in the Sa'dah region but also in seizing control of the Yemeni government in Sana'a. Questions regarding the surprising success of the Houthi military were partially answered when their militias were found armed with heavy weaponry formerly used by Saleh's Republican Guards. Only after the release of a leaked phone conversation in October 2014 between Saleh and Houthi field commander 'Abdulwahid Abu Ras did the public finally receive confirmation of what many had come to suspect—that Saleh had sold his country into the hands of a rebel group who were now targeting his former political opponents. Prior to relinquishing power in 2011, Saleh had begun colluding with the Houthis, believing that an alliance between the two mortal enemies would be politically expedient for both sides. Until his murder in December 2017, Saleh maintained a strong political position in Yemen and was still the ultimate kingmaker.

What were the long-term causes of the current conflict?

Before becoming a potent military and political force, the Houthi movement was primarily a religious organization dedicated to Zaydi revivalism in the face of Salafi proselytization, an theological shift supported by the Yemeni republic since its creation. Beginning in the 1990s, tensions between Zaydi groups and the Saudi-financed spread of Salafi organizations festered unabated. Rather than intervene, Saleh used these religious differences to his advantage by sending Ali Muhsin, his longtime friend and political rival, as well as a supporter of Salafi ideology, to conduct the Sa'dah wars in 2004. When Saleh was forced from power in 2011, an obstacle was eliminated from the path of the Zaydi revivalist movement's struggle against the spread of the Yemeni state-sponsored Salafi ideology. The Houthi expansion after 2011 took on traits of a sectarian struggle as field commanders targeted the Dar al-Hadith center in Dammaj and the network of Salafi schools whose teaching had been responsible for the dissemination of radical Sunni Islamic ideology. One of the first targets of the Houthi militia on arriving in Sana'a in September 2014 was the campus of al-Iman University, an ultra-conservative Sunni institution, responsible for the radicalization of its many graduates.

Religious tensions between Zaydis and Salafis in recent decades were compounded by the decades-long political, social, and economic marginalization of the country's northern population. Since the 1960s, sayyid families had been replaced at the top of the social hierarchy by a new tribal and republican elite. In retribution for their northern support of the deposed imam during the 1960s civil war, the republic consciously withheld resources for education, health, and infrastructure development. The new republic adopted the Salafi ideology of Muhammad Shawkani, a 19th-century Yemeni scholar, as a way to cleanse the country from centuries of Zaydi religious rule and social hierarchy. Aside from limited political representation offered by the Hizb al-Haq Party during the 1990s and the post-Arab Spring Hizb al-Umma Party in 2012, the northern Zaydi population generally and Houthi supporters in particular were not well represented in Yemen's parliament and their grievances were overshadowed by more organized and wealthy tribal leaders. The final political insult occurred at the hands of Hadi and the transitional government who reduced fuel subsidies in July 2014 and pushed forward a plan to divide Yemen into a federal state of six-region. Both of Hadi's initiatives disproportionally targeted supporters of the Houthi movement. Abdul Malek al-Houthi openly criticized what he perceived as the government's strategy of provocation, and called upon collective public displeasure to fuel the Houthi momentum that carried the movement all the way to the capital city of Sana'a.

What has been the humanitarian impact of the bombing campaign and blockade?

The international media continue to focus significant attention on the growing humanitarian crisis in Yemen. International humanitarian aid topped $3 billion in 2019, responding to well-publicized outbreaks of cholera, diphtheria, and other water- and mosquito-borne diseases. It is indeed difficult to see a starving child and not feel immediate sympathy and outrage at the perpetrators of violence. Yemen, however, has been on the brink of a famine for the past decade as poor government planning, insufficient infrastructure, and a growing population have combined to create a looming disaster, made exponentially worse by the new onset of hostilities and Saudi Arabia's blockade of the country.

Before the start of the Saudi air campaign in 2015, more than half of Yemen's children were chronically malnourished. The country's demographic problem is one of the worst in the world, as a 3.2% annual population growth leads to unsustainably high rates of unemployment and a growing strain on the country's water, food, and medical resources. In 2010, Yemeni families were spending between 55% and 70% of their household income on food, water, and energy, a consequence of high prices, insufficient salaries, and reported unemployment rates as high as 70%. Despite the size of Yemen's agricultural economy and workforce, the country is dependent on imported food for 90% of its wheat consumption and 100% of its rice.

The exponential increases in appeals for humanitarian aid have exacerbated the conflict by unintentionally financing the belligerent parties, who use military strength to seize control of foreign aid shipments. Humanitarian aid has quickly become the largest economic sector in the country., In 2019 alone, over $3 billion in international aid was delivered, constituting nearly 10% of Yemen's pre-war GDP. One-third of the aid budget is financed by Saudi Arabia and the United Arab Emirates (UAE), while Western countries have been covering the rest. Dumping humanitarian supplies on the shores of Yemen has become a form of absolution for Saudi and Emirati aggression and for international failures to intervene in a meaningful way to address the roots of the conflict rather than their symptoms. It is impossible to trace the movement of aid once delivered in Yemen, leaving to speculation the amount of food, water, and medicine that actually gets delivered to those most in need. Reports from Sana'a and other beleaguered cities complain about the exorbitant prices being charged in local stores for the humanitarian aid given to the Yemeni people free of charge.

In 2020, there were 12 international organizations with active humanitarian aid programs in Yemen supporting areas such as health, nutrition, and hygiene. These organizations have no clear exit strategy from Yemen as the donor countries have failed to establish safeguards against unhealthy dependency by local and national institutions. Rather than focusing on building capacity and retaining locally trained professionals, humanitarian organizations have distributed funds according to donors' priorities and politics, and have relied primarily on costly foreign staff. As a result, basic preventative healthcare has suffered at the expense of well-funded foreign programs addressing individual diseases or outbreaks.

Perhaps one of the reasons the humanitarian situation in Yemen did not receive international attention prior to 2017 is that there has not been a Syria-like refugee crisis as a result of the violence and shortage of food and other necessities. The same geography that placed Yemen at the center of the Indian Ocean and Red Sea trade for centuries has limited the mobility of millions of internally displaced refugees. Surrounded on two sides by water and on two sides by vast deserts, Yemenis literally have nowhere to go. Oman, Yemen's neighbor to the east, welcomed a mere 5,000 refugees in 2017, turning away thousands of others at its tightly controlled border. Saudi Arabia, which shares the longest border with Yemen, is unlikely to set up refugee camps across its southern border, at least not while it continues to carry out the bombing campaign that has precipitated Yemen's internal refugee crisis. The continued construction of a border wall along the Saudi-Yemeni border will not make the movement of populations any easier.

What happened to Yemen's ousted government?

Many Yemeni protesters of the Arab Spring and the old political stalwarts alike were disappointed by the appointment of Hadi as interim president in 2012. Hadi has spent his career running away from confrontation and preferring to avoid Yemen during times of conflict and political turmoil. Born in the South Yemen governorate of Abyan, Hadi left to study abroad during the 1960s while both North and South Yemen were undergoing revolutions that transformed South Arabia. He stayed abroad studying military tactics and leadership in Egypt and the Soviet Union during the 1970s, before returning to the socialist PDRY to assume senior military positions. During the PDRY civil war in 1986, Hadi fled north with Ali Nasser Muhammad and even sided with Ali Abdullah Saleh during the 1994 civil war, which earned him the position of vice president from 1994 to 2012. When the Houthis captured Sana'a in September 2014, eventually placing Hadi under house arrest, he managed to escape the capital city in February 2015, dragging the Houthi tribal militias behind him as he fled to Aden. In March 2015, when the Houthis reached Aden, leaving a trail of destruction in their wake, Hadi again chose flight over fight and left Aden for Saudi Arabia.

What was initially supposed to be a temporary position turned into a permanent presidency as Hadi resettled in Riyadh, Saudi Arabia, and asked for Saudi military assistance in combating the Houthi militias. Overnight, Hadi managed to convince the Saudi royal family and the world that he remained Yemen's legitimate ruler, despite the fact that his jurisdiction consisted of several luxury hotel rooms in Saudi Arabia. This led to many unfortunate jokes about the Hadi regime in Riyadh, including one that ridiculed the appointment of new ministers in a government with no administrative responsibilities. As the joke went, when Hadi swore in new ministers, they did not take an oath of allegiance to the Yemeni state, but rather promised to keep the hotel clean and not to lose their room key!

Periodic news reports display photos of Hadi triumphantly returning to Aden to administer a government out of Yemen's second capital. What the images do not display is the number of security personnel surrounding Hadi and the countless Saudi and Emirati mercenaries who reconquered Aden and its environs on Hadi's behalf. Nor do news reports provide full details of the disparate groups that make up Hadi's "coalition forces," highlighted by the fact that in January 2018, the UAE-supported Southern Transitional Council (STC) took over government offices in what Hadi's prime minister, Ahmed Obeid bin Daghr, called a coup. Unsurprisingly, at the first sign of resistance, Hadi returned to the relative safety of his Riyadh hotel room. Replacing Hadi has become even more difficult as he took the politically expedient action of appointing as his vice president Ali Muhsin al-Ahmar, an open supporter of Islah, an alternative that would only further infuriate the Houthis and test Hadi's relations with the United States and other Western countries. For the time being, the international community is stuck with the Hadi government, which is recognized by every country except one—Yemen.

The signing of the Riyadh Agreement in November 2019 was supposed to give Hadi's government the lifeline they so desperately needed by forming a union with the STC in South Yemen. What Hadi hoped would be interpreted by the STC as a tacit approval of his federalist plan for Yemen turned into a southern declaration of independence and an STC rejection of Hadi's Riyadh government. As the STC popularity has increased and Hadramawt has continued to exercise a greater degree of autonomy, Hadi is relegated once again as a president without a land and increasingly without a people.

What happened to the rest of Saleh's family?

When Ali Abdullah Saleh was killed in December 2017 by his former Houthi allies, public attention immediately turned to other members of the Saleh family under the assumption that one or more of them might try to seize the family position of leadership. His nephew Tareq Saleh, who led the Yemeni army's elite Republican Guard, mysteriously went missing until January 2018, reemerging with a public video declaring his newfound opposition to the Houthi movement after three years of fighting alongside his uncle. In response, the UAE helped Tareq reestablish a small army near Ta'iz where he began a renewed but ultimately unsuccessful military campaign. By early 2020, even the Saudis had warmed to the idea of supporting the former president's nephew and were willing to overlook three years of Tareq's fighting against Saudi forces in Yemen (2015–2017) in the hope that his family name was still worth something to Yemenis in a potential reconquest of Sana'a. Tareq's growing supporters, fueled by a armed group of 20,000 known as the Joint Forces, continue to factor into decisions made by both Riyadh and Abu Dhabi.

Ahmed Ali, the former president's eldest son, was once thought of as the Saleh family successor as president. Unfortunately, Ahmed had the misfortune of being in Abu Dhabi in 2015 when his father made public his alliance with the Houthis, leading to Ahmed's suspected house arrest, which was only lifted after he formally denounced the Houthi movement in December 2017. Ahmed Ali still maintains residence in the Emirates, occasionally making a public appearance but largely living the life of a playboy, taking advantage of the influence and fortune still associated with his family name. His younger brother Khalid is said to be living in the Emirates as well. Salah and Maydan Saleh, two of the former president's other sons, were released from Houthi captivity in October 2018 after a ransom was reportedly paid. Neither of them appears regularly in public nor does the rest of the Saleh family, who managed to flee to Aden shortly after Ali Abdullah's death.

As neither Tareq nor Ahmed Ali has managed to secure the remnants of the GPC, the brainchild political party of Ali Abdullah Saleh, it remains fragmented into three factions. Tareq, and occasionally Ahmed Ali, represent one segment of the GPC which is both anti-Saudi and anti-Houthi. Those members of the GPC who still reside in Sana'a, have little choice but to offer rhetorical support to the Houthi movement. Mansur Hadi and his government represent the third component of the former GPC, leading a government in exile in open contention with the other two groups.

Will South Yemen declare independence?

When street protests broke out across Yemen in 2011 as part of the Arab Spring movement, this was not a new occurrence in Aden, where continuous street protests had been taking place since 2007. The mass protests across South Yemen were part of the popular movement known as al-Hirak al-Junubi, or the Southern Movement. Al-Hirak was a manifestation of growing southern discontent with northern dominance that had been simmering since the end of the 1994 North-South civil war. By 2011, the old southern flag of the People's Democratic Republic of Yemen was a ubiquitous symbol flying over homes and business in Aden—a clear popular expression of southern calls for independence. What had begun as a peaceful movement was transformed into a fierce armed resistance in March 2015 as southerners fought against the invading Houthi-Saleh alliance and with Emirati support, Aden was "liberated."

Over the next two years, Hadi tried to consolidate political control over the South, even as growing elements within its population supported the idea of southern self-rule. Growing public protests against Hadi's government in Aden had culminated with the creation of the Southern Transitional Council (STC) in May 2017, by a group of former al-Hirak leaders, headed by Aidroos al-Zubaydi, the former governor of Aden who had been fired by Hadi. Among the STC leadership is also a Salafi named Hani Bin Breik who has developed a degree of popularity among southerners for his 2015 defense of Aden in the face of Houthi fighters and for his vocal anti-Saudi agenda. The UAE-supported STC formed its own shadow cabinet and ministries, openly clashing with the Saudi-supported Hadi government. In a last-ditch effort to avoid the collapse of southern governance, Hadi and the STC leadership signed the Riyadh Agreement in November 2019, seen as a union between the two redundant governing institutions. The Riyadh Agreement collapsed shortly thereafter as the two sides reached differing interpretations, with Hadi hoping for a federal state in Yemen while the STC had every intention of declaring an independent South Yemen. Even as the STC has emerged as a political alternative to Mansur Hadi's government in Aden, officially declaring their independence in April 2020, there still remain significant segments of the southern and Hadrami populations that maintain an open preference for Hadi's